impact

1

SERIES EDITORS
JoAnn (Jodi) Crandall
Joan Kang Shin

AUTHOR
Lesley Koustaff

NATIONAL GEOGRAPHIC LEARNING | CENGAGE Learning

Australia • Brazil • Mexico • Singapore • United Kingdom • United States

Thank you to the educators who provided invaluable feedback during the development of *Impact*:

EXPERT PANEL

Márcia Ferreira, Academic Coordinator, CCBEU, Franca, Brazil

Jianwei Song, Vice-general Manager, Ensure International Education, Harbin, China

María Eugenia Flores, Academic Director, and **Liana Rojas-Binda**, Head of Recruitment & Training, Centro Cultural Costarricense-Norteamericano, San José, Costa Rica

Liani Setiawati, M.Pd., SMPK 1 BPK PENABUR Bandung, Bandung, Indonesia

Micaela Fernandes, Head of Research and Development Committee and Assessment Committee, Pui Ching Middle School, Macau

Héctor Sánchez Lozano, Academic Director, and **Carolina Tripodi**, Head of the Juniors Program, Proulex, Guadalajara, Mexico

Rosario Giraldez, Academic Director, Alianza Cultural, Montevideo, Uruguay

REVIEWERS

BRAZIL

Renata Cardoso, Colégio do Sol, Guara, DF

Fábio Delano Vidal Carneiro, Colégio Sete de Setembro, Fortaleza

Cristiano Carvalho, Centro Educacional Leonardo da Vinci, Vitória

Silvia Corrêa, Associação Alumni, São Paulo

Carol Espinosa, Associação Cultural Brasil Estados Unidos, Salvador

Marcia Ferreira, Centro Cultural Brasil Estados Unidos, Franca

Clara Haddad, ELT Consultant, São Paulo

Elaine Carvalho Chaves Hodgson, Colégio Militar de Brasília, Brasília

Thays Farias Galvão Ladosky, Associação Brasil América, Recife

Itana Lins, Colégio Anchieta, Salvador

Samantha Mascarenhas, Associação Cultural Brasil Estados Unidos, Salvador

Ann Marie Moreira, Pan American School of Bahia, Bahia

Rodrigo Ramirez, CEETEPS- Fatec Zona Sul, São Paulo

Paulo Torres, Vitória Municipality, Vitória

Renata Zainotte, Go Up Idiomas, Rio de Janeiro

CHINA

Zhou Chao, MaxEn Education, Beijing

Zhu Haojun, Only International Education, Shanghai

Su Jing, Beijing Chengxun International English School, Beijing

Jianjun Shen, Phoenix City International School, Guangzhou

COSTA RICA

Luis Antonio Quesada-Umaña, Centro Cultural Costarricense Norteamericano, San José

INDONESIA

Luz S. Ismail, M.A., LIA Institute of Language and Vocational Training, Jakarta

Selestin Zainuddin, LIA Institute of Language and Vocational Training, Jakarta

Rosalia Dian Devitasari, SMP Kolese Kanisius, Jakarta

JAPAN

John Williams, Tezukayama Gakuen, Nara

MEXICO

Nefertiti González, Instituto Mexicano Madero, Puebla

Eugenia Islas, Instituto Tlalpan, Mexico City

Marta MM Seguí, Colegio Velmont A.C., Puebla

SOUTH KOREA

Min Yuol (Alvin) Cho, Global Leader English Education, Yong In

THAILAND

Panitnan Kalayanapong, Eduzone Co., Ltd., Bangkok

TURKEY

Damla Çaltuğ, İELEV, Istanbul

Basak Nalcakar Demiralp, Ankara Sinav College, Ankara

Humeyra Olcayli, İstanbul Bilim College, Istanbul

VIETNAM

Chantal Kruger, ILA Vietnam, Hô Chí Minh

Ai Nguyen Huynh, Vietnam USA Society, Hô Chí Minh

impact

1

1 **Life in the City** p. 8	**2** **Amazing Jobs** p. 24	**3** **Secrets of the Dark** p. 42	**4** **Living Together** p. 58
THEME			
Exploring your city or town	Unusual and interesting careers	The world at night	Animal and human interaction
VOCABULARY STRATEGIES			
· Prefix *un-* · Use context	· Suffixes *-er*, *-or*, and *-ist* · Identify word parts (suffixes)	· Compound words · Use a dictionary: Most common meaning	· Prefix *mis-* · Identify collocations
SPEAKING STRATEGY			
Active listening	Extending the conversation	Asking for help and helping with schoolwork	Asking for and giving reasons
GRAMMAR			
Simple present: Talking about facts *I live near the High Line.* **In and on:** Expressing location *Lion City is in eastern China.*	**Simple present questions and answers:** Talking about routines *Do pastry chefs work every day? Yes, they do. / No, they don't.* **Possessives:** Showing ownership *This dentist's job isn't done in an office.*	**Present progressive:** Saying what is happening now *While I'm reading in bed at night in Mexico, my friend Akiko is reading at school in Japan!* **At, on, and in:** Saying when things happen *at eight o'clock, on Monday(s), in the winter*	**Modals:** Describing obligation and advice *We have to protect rhinos. We shouldn't ignore the rhino problem.* **Modals:** Describing ability in present and past *What can we do about it? How could they avoid cars?*
READING			
A New Type of Park	*Adventures Near and Far*	*In the Dark of the Ocean*	*Four-legged Heroes*
READING STRATEGY			
Make predictions	Compare and contrast	Scan the text	Identify problems and solutions
VIDEO			
Mission Re-Wild	*Searching for Life in Iceland's Fissures*	*What Glows Beneath*	*The Elephant Whisperers*
WRITING			
Genre: **Descriptive paragraph** Focus: Use adjectives	Genre: **Descriptive paragraph** Focus: Identify and include elements of a paragraph	Genre: **Descriptive paragraph** Focus: Use sensory writing	Genre: **Descriptive paragraph** Focus: Proofread
MISSION			
Explore Your World National Geographic Explorer: **Daniel Raven-Ellison**, Guerilla Geographer	**Do What You Love** National Geographic Explorer: **Guillermo de Anda**, Underwater Archaeologist	**Understand and Protect** National Geographic Explorer: **David Gruber**, Marine Biologist	**Start Small** National Geographic Explorer: **Amy Dickman**, Animal Conservationist
PRONUNCIATION			
Syllables and stress	Intonation in questions	Present progressive: Stress of the verb *be*	*Can* and *can't*
EXPRESS YOURSELF			
Creative Expression: **Travel review** *Gondola Tours of Venice* Making connections: Unusual places and unusual jobs		Creative Expression: **Graphic story** *Sleeping with a Lion* Making connections: Interactions between humans and animals at night	

Unit 1

DANIEL RAVEN-ELLISON **Guerrilla Geographer**

Daniel Raven-Ellison believes that guerrilla geography helps you to see the world around you in new ways. Daniel explores urban areas. He has walked across many cities, taking a picture after every eight steps! Daniel wants everyone to get outdoors, explore, and discover the surprises that the world has for us.

Unit 2

GUILLERMO DE ANDA **Underwater Archaeologist**

Guillermo de Anda explores caves in the Yucatán Peninsula in Mexico, sometimes for more than 12 hours at a time. He's searching for artifacts from the Mayan civilization. When he explores, Guillermo faces challenges like swimming in small spaces and dodging swarms of bats. Would you enjoy this unusual job?

Unit 3

DAVID GRUBER **Marine Biologist**

David Gruber has always loved the ocean. When he was a teenager, he learned to surf. While he surfed, he wondered what was below the waves. Now David is a marine biologist. He studies underwater animals that make their own light. David wants to understand these incredible creatures and why they glow.

Unit 4

AMY DICKMAN **Animal Conservationist**

When Amy Dickman was young, she wanted to work with big cats. Today, as an animal conservationist, she does just that! Amy works in Tanzania giving talks, meeting local villagers, and helping people understand how to live with and help big cats. Amy thinks small actions, such as talking to others about endangered animals, can make a big difference.

Unit 5

ANDRÉS RUZO Geoscientist

Andrés Ruzo grew up between Nicaragua, Peru, and Texas. As a boy in Lima, Peru, he heard a legend about a boiling river. He is now the first geoscientist given permission to study that boiling river. His work can be dangerous. A local shaman told him, "Use your feet like eyes." You can't see heat, but you can feel it when you step near it. So Andrés wore sandals!

Unit 6

JOSH PONTE Musical Explorer/Filmmaker

Josh Ponte mixes traditional music with new music inspired by his travels to Gabon. Josh is helping to preserve the traditional music and dance of Gabon, much of which is disappearing. By mixing traditional music with new music, Josh is helping new generations to keep their traditions alive.

Unit 7

MANU PRAKASH Biophysicist

As a child, Manu Prakash enjoyed experimenting in an empty chemistry lab. Now he's a biophysicist who has his own lab at Stanford University. Manu believes everyone should be able to understand science. That's why he created the Foldscope, a paper microscope. He hopes that this inexpensive tool will allow more people, especially young people, to make discoveries.

Unit 8

ALBERTO NAVA BLANK Underwater Cave Explorer/Cartographer

Alberto Nava Blank dives deep into the underwater caves near Tulum, Mexico, to learn about the past. In 2007, Alberto and his team discovered the thirteen-thousand-year-old skeleton of a young girl. From this discovery, researchers have been able to learn more about how our human ancestors migrated from Asia, across the Pacific, and through the Americas.

Life in the City

"Geography is about curiosity, exploration, and discovery. It gives you the power to see places in new ways, search for your own answers, and make sense of the world."

—Daniel Raven-Ellison

A red fox exploring Bristol, UK

1. Look at the photo. If you saw this in person, would it surprise you? Why or why not?

2. The animal in the photo is exploring. Do you explore? Why is it good to explore a new place?

3. What is your favorite place? What do you do there? Why is this place special to you?

9

1 **What makes Astana different from other cities?** Discuss. Then listen and read. TR: 2

The city of Astana is truly a **unique** place. It was **constructed** in 1997 to replace the city of Almaty as the **capital** of Kazakhstan. Almaty was in the southeastern corner of the country, but the president of Kazakhstan wanted a new capital. So Astana was built right in the middle of the country. As a result, this modern city is **surrounded by** nothing but rural areas.

The unusual **architecture** of Astana makes it look like a space-age city. There are amazing **skyscrapers** and eye-catching buildings. A cultural center looks like a big, blue eye. A university building has the **shape** of a dog bowl.

The Bayterek Tower in downtown Astana

Another unusual building, the Bayterek **Tower**, is a **symbol** of the city. This tall structure is 105 m (345 ft.) high, and looks like an enormous tree with a golden egg inside.

A Japanese architect named Kisho Kurokawa won first prize in a competition to **design** and **plan** the new capital. He included many parks and public spaces to connect urban life with nature.

Astana has pleasant summers. But the weather can get very cold in the winter, with temperatures dropping to -40°C (-40°F). Because of its extreme climate, Astana offers a lot of **indoor** entertainment. A popular entertainment center is the Khan Shatyr, or king's tent, the world's largest tent. Inside there is a river for boating, a park, an indoor running track, a waterslide, and even a sandy beach with palm trees! The **residents** of Astana can enjoy a variety of outdoor activities even when it's well below freezing.

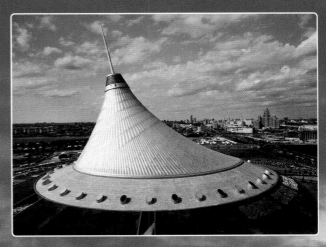

The Khan Shatyr

2 **Learn new words.** Listen and repeat. TR: 3

3 **Work in pairs.** Compare Astana to the place where you live. What do you like and dislike about each place? Would you like to live in Astana? Why or why not?

4 Read and write the words from the list. Make any necessary changes.

architecture	capital	outdoor	plan
resident	skyscraper	surrounded by	unique

Daniel Raven-Ellison has a very _____ job: he's a guerrilla geographer. He loves exploring places and making discoveries. Daniel says that we are _____ interesting things just waiting to be discovered. According to him, _____ of a place should keep exploring. They can make new discoveries even if they've lived in the same place their whole lives. Daniel _____ all kinds of exciting adventures. In one adventure, he climbed more than 3,300 floors of the many tall _____ in London. In another, he walked across Mexico City, the _____ of Mexico. He photographed everything he saw in front of him every eight steps. He took photos of _____ , streets, and public spaces. He's done the same thing in twelve other cities!

5 Learn new words. Listen for these words and match them with the definitions. Then listen and repeat. **TR: 4 and 5**

rural	unusual	urban

_____ 1. different or uncommon

_____ 2. relating to the countryside

_____ 3. relating to the city

Daniel Raven-Ellison

6 Choose an activity.

1. **Work independently.** Go on a discovery walk outdoors. Find things that are hard, soft, sticky, brown, pink, small, big, or smelly. Take photos and present your experience to the class.

2. **Work in pairs.** Think of two adventures you can have near your home. Why would you choose these adventures? What can you learn from them?

3. **Work independently.** Walk through your school building and take photographs every eight steps. What interesting things do you see? Create a photo book of your discoveries.

SPEAKING STRATEGY TR: 6

Active listening

Really?	You're kidding!
Wow!	Seriously?
No way!	That's <u>incredible</u>!

7 **Listen.** How do the speakers show they're listening actively? Write the words and phrases you hear. TR: 7

8 **Read and complete the dialogue.**

Dad: Meiling, look at this. I found this old map of our city. It's more than 100 years old.

Meiling: _____ Let me see.

Dad: This building was a hospital. It's a music hall now.

Meiling: _____

Dad: I know! And this was the old library.

Meiling: _____ Now it's a tall skyscraper.

Dad: And look. This was a park.

Meiling: _____ It's my school now!

Dad: Hey, let's take a walk. We can bring the map and look for other changes.

Meiling: Great idea! I'll bring my camera and take some pictures.

9 **Work in groups.** Take turns. Choose a card. Read the question and the possible answers. Group members guess the correct answer and use active listening to respond to the real answer.

One million?
That's amazing!

How many ants are there for every person in the world?
A. one thousand
B. one million
C. six million

B. one million

Go to p. 153.

10 **Work in pairs.** Think of an interesting place, thing, or event in your neighborhood, and describe it to your partner. Your partner should use the words and phrases above to show active listening. When you finish, switch roles.

Simple present: Talking about facts

I **live** near the High Line.
She **works** next to the High Line.
Cars **don't drive** on the High Line.

You **go** to concerts on the High Line.
The High Line **doesn't allow** pets.
We **walk** through the High Line's gardens.

11 **Listen.** You will hear eight facts about the High Line. For each fact, circle the simple present form you hear. TR: 9

1. grow   grows   don't grow
2. visit   visits   doesn't visit
3. open   opens   doesn't open
4. close   closes   doesn't close

5. need   needs   don't need
6. enjoy   enjoys   don't enjoy
7. sell   sells   doesn't sell
8. get   gets   don't get

12 **Read.** Complete the sentences with the correct simple-present form of the verbs in parentheses.

1. The High Line _____ open all night. (not stay)

2. The High Line _____ special chairs for relaxing. (have)

3. A tour guide _____ about the High Line's gardens. (talk)

4. Musicians _____ concerts on Saturday afternoons. (give)

5. Visitors _____ to walk along the High Line. (not pay)

13 **Work in pairs.** Take turns saying facts about the High Line. Use the simple present.

1. the High Line / have / a play area for children
2. you / not / need / a ticket for the High Line
3. many different animals / live / on the High Line
4. guides / give / free tours to visitors
5. he / attend / exercise classes on the High Line
6. I / want / to visit the High Line

The High Line in
New York City, USA

14 **Learn new words.** Read about the Cheonggyecheon Stream park in Seoul, Korea. Then listen and repeat. TR: 10 and 11

bridge

sidewalk

stream

Cheonggyecheon Stream

In 2003, the mayor of Seoul decided to remove a **highway** over an underground **stream**. He wanted the area around the stream to be an urban green space for people to enjoy. Today the six-kilometer (four-mile) park on either side of the Cheonggyecheon Stream provides a place for people to relax.

At the park, visitors attend traditional festivals and concerts. They enjoy cultural events, look at art, and watch water and light shows. Many people just walk along the **sidewalks** or over one of 22 **bridges**, each with its own design and meaning.

15 **Read and complete the sentences.** Make any necessary changes.

bridge	highway	sidewalk	stream

1. The Cheonggyecheon Stream was covered by a _____ .

2. Now visitors take walks on the _____ near the water.

3. People enjoy water shows over the _____ .

4. Each of the _____ has a unique look and meaning.

16 **Work in groups.** Name an interesting outdoor place where you live. How do people enjoy this place? What do you see and do at this place? Use the simple present.

17 **Before you read, discuss in pairs.** Look at the title and the photo. What do you think the reading is about?

18 **Learn new words.** Look at the words below. What do you think they mean?

concrete	land	outdoor	park

Now find them in the reading. Has your idea about the meaning changed? Explain. Then listen and repeat. TR: 12

19 **While you read, look for words and phrases that support your prediction.** TR: 13

20 **After you read, look at the sentences.** Check T for *true* or F for *false*.

1. London is now a national park city. Ⓣ Ⓕ

2. London has 13,000 parks. Ⓣ Ⓕ

3. London has a lot of green spaces. Ⓣ Ⓕ

4. Most children in London spend their days playing outside. Ⓣ Ⓕ

5. Daniel wants people to spend more time outdoors. Ⓣ Ⓕ

A New Type of Park

Can the capital of England become a national park?

Imagine stepping out your front door and standing in the middle of a national park. Daniel Raven-Ellison hopes this might soon be possible for millions of London residents. Daniel is leading a campaign to make London a national park city.

Although London has much more concrete than a national park usually would, it is home to more than 13,000 kinds of wildlife. These species live in its 3,000 parks, along with 1,500 varieties of flowering plants, and more than 300 species of birds. In fact, 47 percent of the land in London is green space.

"We have eight million trees in London; it's the world's largest urban forest," Daniel says. That's almost one tree for every person living in London! Yet, even though London has thousands of outdoor spaces, one in seven children living there hasn't visited a green space in the past year.

Daniel believes that making London into a national park will protect the animal life and green spaces in London. He hopes it will also encourage people, especially young people, to spend more time outdoors. Daniel takes his own son out to explore in London, and he thinks that other parents should do the same. Daniel is convinced that people who spend a lot of time in nature live happier and healthier lives. What do you think?

21 **Check your predictions.** Look at your predictions from Activity 17. Were you correct? What surprised you in this reading?

22 **Discuss in groups.**

1. How often do you visit green spaces? In your opinion, is it enough? What things do you do there?

2. Do you think that turning your city into a national park would be good? Why or why not?

3. Imagine that you can make changes in your city. Which places do you want to protect? Which places do you want to change? How do you want to change them? Explain your answers.

23 **Before you watch, guess how much green space each place has.** Draw a line to match the percentage to the city.

1. Seoul, Korea   2.3%
2. Hong Kong, China   2.5%
3. Mumbai, India   4.4%
4. Bogotá, Colombia   41%
5. Moscow, Russia   47%
6. Singapore   54%

24 **Read and circle.** You're going to watch *Mission Re-Wild*. From the title and the photo, predict what the video is about. Circle the letter.

a. Putting wild animals back into forests
b. Building more skyscrapers in cities
c. Making more green space in cities

25 Watch scene 1.1. **While you watch, check your guesses from Activity 23.** How many were correct?

A mural made from moss by artist Carly Schmitt

26 **After you watch, read the sentences.** Circle the correct answer.

1. Cities with *a lot of* / *very little* green space are sometimes called *concrete jungles.*

2. Seoul and Mumbai have *a lot of* / *very little* green space.

3. People who spend time outdoors are *happier* / *unhappier* than people who don't.

4. You can enjoy the outdoors *in both rural and urban areas* / *only in rural areas.*

5. *Only some cities have* / *Every city has* signs of natural life.

6. One way to start re-wilding is *planting a tree* / *recycling plastic.*

27 **Work in pairs.** Put the steps for re-wilding a city in the correct order.

_____ Birds build nests in the tree.

___1___ Plant a seed in the ground.

_____ People like seeing the tree and the birds.

_____ The seed grows into a small tree.

_____ Other people begin to plant trees, too.

28 **Discuss in pairs.**

1. How much public green space is there where you live? Would you like more? Why or why not?

2. Why do you think some places have more public green space than other places?

29 **Choose an activity.**

1. **Work independently.** Imagine you're going to re-wild a space where you live. Where is it? How will you do it? Make a plan and present it to the class.

2. **Work in pairs.** Find out about a place that was successfully re-wilded. How did it change? How do people enjoy it now? Write a paragraph and use photos to tell what you learned.

3. **Work in groups.** Prepare a "Let's Re-Wild" poster to teach others about re-wilding. Write three reasons why it is good to re-wild. Write ideas on what people can do. Draw pictures of a space before and after it has been re-wilded.

GRAMMAR TR: 14

In and *on*: Expressing location

Lion City is **in** eastern China.

There are many beautiful bridges **in** Lion City.

Lion City is **in** the water.

China is **on** the continent of Asia.

Lion City is one of the most unique places **on** Earth.

Lion City is not **on** a mountain.

30 **Listen.** Write *in* or *on* in the spaces below. **TR: 15**

1. There are many ancient cities _____ Asia, such as Shi Cheng, also known as Lion City.

2. Shi Cheng is an ancient city located _____ China.

3. Visitors to Shi Cheng today can't walk _____ its streets to admire it.

4. It isn't _____ a mountain or _____ an island. It's _____ the water!

5. _____ Shi Cheng, there are 265 archways crossing over its streets.

6. There are beautiful sculptures of lions, dragons, and birds _____ these archways.

31 **Work in pairs.** Listen to the passage again. Write two additional facts about Shi Cheng. Use *on* and *in* in your sentences. **TR: 16**

_____

_____

32 **Work in groups.** Take turns using the spinner. Make sentences using *in* or *on*.

About seven billion people live on Earth.

Go to p. 155.

20

In descriptive writing, we try to create a picture for the reader. We use describing words to help the reader clearly imagine what we're writing about. Examples of describing words include:

beautiful   **colorful**   **new**   **short**   **sweet-smelling**   **yellow**

33 **Read the model.** Work in pairs to find and underline all of the describing words the writer uses to tell about the garden.

   Last year the empty lot across from my bus stop was a sad, empty, ugly space, with only a couple of dead bushes and one short tree. Then some hard-working gardeners in the neighborhood changed that. They were tired of looking at that sad space while waiting for the bus, so they made it into a beautiful garden. Now on a sunny summer day you can look across the street and see colorful vegetable plants and sweet-smelling flowers while you wait for the bus. Yellow butterflies fly from plant to plant, and tiny birds sing in the green trees. I love taking the bus now!

34 **Work in pairs.** Draw a picture of the garden described in Activity 33. Compare your drawing with a partner's. How are they the same? How are they different?

35 **Write.** Think of a beautiful place in your neighborhood. Use describing words to write a paragraph about this place.

Explore Your World

"There are amazing adventures to be had right outside our doors."

—Daniel Raven-Ellison

National Geographic Explorer, Guerrilla Geographer

1. Watch scene 1.2.

2. Daniel thinks it's best for students to experience geography rather than just read about it. What other school subjects can you explore outside the classroom? How can you explore them?

3. How much of your town or city have you explored? What else is there to learn about where you live? Keep a journal of outdoor adventures you have in your area.

Make an Impact

A **Conduct a survey.**

· Ask your friends how much time they spent indoors and outdoors in the past week.

· Calculate the average amount of indoor and outdoor time.

· Present your findings to the class. Give suggestions for spending more time outdoors.

B **Plan and conduct a scavenger hunt.**

· Work as a group to prepare a list of items to find in a local green space.

· Work independently to find the items on the list.

· Discuss which items on the list were the easiest and the most difficult to find.

C **Write a newspaper article.**

· Think of someone who has lived in your neighborhood for a long time. Write questions to ask about.

· Interview that person. Find maps and photos to show the changes that he or she describes.

· Write a newspaper article to summarize the interview and show the changes.

Amazing Jobs

NASA astronauts working underwater on a
Hubble space telescope model

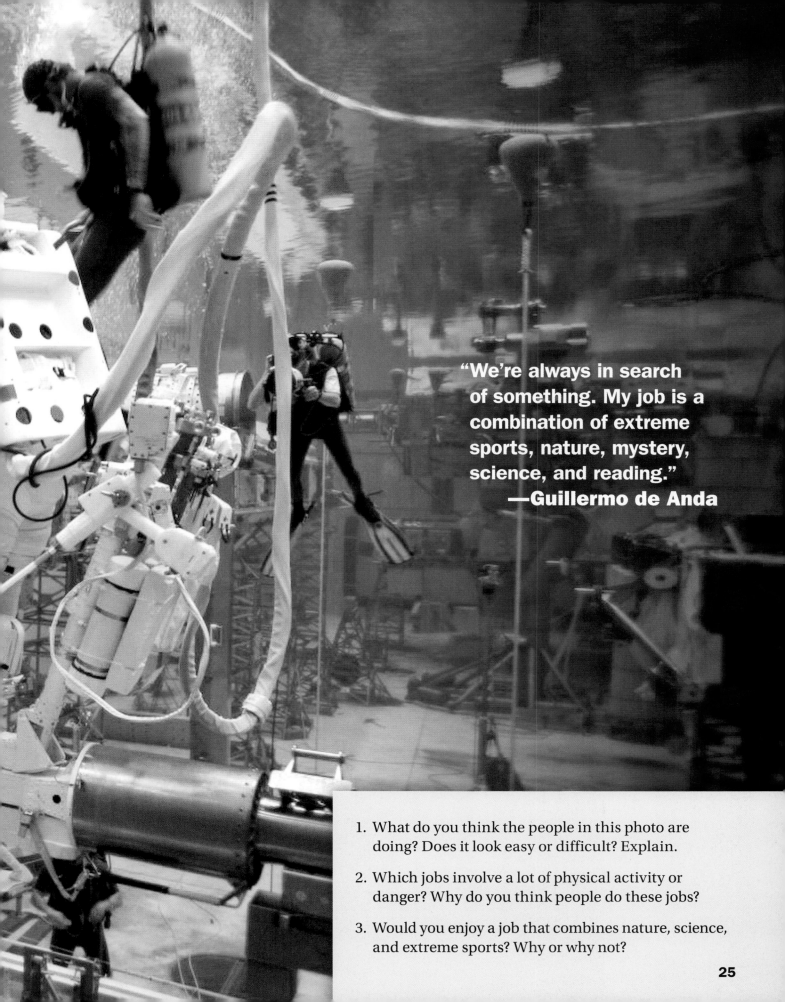

"We're always in search of something. My job is a combination of extreme sports, nature, mystery, science, and reading."
—Guillermo de Anda

1. What do you think the people in this photo are doing? Does it look easy or difficult? Explain.

2. Which jobs involve a lot of physical activity or danger? Why do you think people do these jobs?

3. Would you enjoy a job that combines nature, science, and extreme sports? Why or why not?

What do underwater **adventure**, detective work, and Mayan history have in common? They're all part of the unusual **profession** of Guillermo de Anda. He's a college professor and an underwater **archaeologist**. Guillermo's **job** is to **explore** flooded underground areas known as *cenotes*. "It's unusual **work** for a lot of people," Guillermo says about his job. "It's hard, but it's a lot of fun as well."

Guillermo dives to learn more about Mayan culture. About 2,000 years ago, the Maya lived in the Yucatán Peninsula of Mexico, the area Guillermo explores. Guillermo dives there now to look for ancient Mayan artifacts underwater. He **studies** them for **clues** about how the Maya lived.

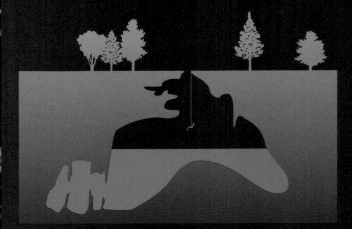

The inside of a cenote

Guillermo doesn't spend all of his time underwater. Like many people, he does much of his work in an **office**. He's also a researcher and a teacher. Sometimes Guillermo takes his archaeology students underwater with him. He wants to **train** them to explore the cenotes. He thinks underwater archaeology is a good **career** choice for his students to **consider**. "Very few archaeologists know how to dive in caves. We need more," he says.

Guillermo and his team are **taking risks** each time they enter a cave. They go over 60 m (200 ft.) underground to dark places filled with bats, snakes, and scorpions. Some of the caves they explore are thousands of meters wide. It's not always easy for the team to remember the way out! Even though it can be dangerous, Guillermo has a **passion** for what he does. "We go back into history when we're in the field," he says. "I never stop learning."

Entering a cenote

2 **Learn new words.** Listen and repeat. TR: 18

3 **Work in pairs.** What makes Guillermo's job unusual? What parts of his job aren't unusual? Would you like to have his job? Why or why not?

4 Read and circle the correct word.

Do you like *adventure* / *profession*? Do you want a job that isn't in *a clue* / *an office*? Do you want to *consider* / *explore* underwater but don't know how to dive? If you answered *yes*, then you might like *a career* / *an archaeologist* as a Remotely Operated Vehicle (ROV) operator.

ROV operators help underwater *archaeologists* / *offices* like Guillermo de Anda. ROV operators help look for *professions* / *clues* about old objects and the people who used them. Explorers like Guillermo also use ROVs to decide what parts of a cave they should explore. Divers *don't study* / *take risks* when they dive into caves, so ROV operators can help them make choices about where to explore. If your *passion* / *career* is exploring, consider becoming an ROV operator.

5 Learn new words. Listen and complete the sentences with the correct word. Then listen and repeat.
TR: 19 and 20

choice	dangerous	researcher

1. If a job is _____ , it isn't safe.

2. When you make a _____ ,
   you decide what you want.

3. A _____ studies people
   or objects to learn more about them.

An ROV

6 Choose an activity.

1. **Work independently.** Think of another use for an ROV. Draw and label your idea. Share it with the class.

2. **Work in pairs.** Imagine you're an underwater archaeologist. What do you like about the job? What don't you like about it? Discuss your ideas with a partner.

3. **Work in groups.** Make a list of five unusual jobs. Ask students in your class which of the jobs they would like to do. Have them explain their answers.

Topic	Extending the conversation
I'd like to be an explorer.	And you? How about you? What do you think?
I can speak Spanish.	Can you?
He knows how to dive.	Do you?

7 **Listen.** How do the speakers extend the conversation? Write the phrases you hear. TR: 22

8 **Read and complete the dialogue.**

Elena: I'd love to work on a cruise ship and travel the world.

_____

Sarah: Not me. The traveling would be fun, but I think it's *really* hard work.

_____

Elena: You're right, it may be hard work. But I like exploring new places.

_____

Sarah: I do, but remember, you have to take care of people. It's not a vacation!

Elena: You're right, but I love people, so it's OK. And I speak Spanish, English, and Mandarin, so I can talk to people from lots of different places.

_____

Sarah: No, I can only speak English. You know, I think I'll be a travel writer. That way, I can travel without taking care of other people!

9 **Work in pairs.** Spin the wheel. Read the sentence aloud, giving correct information about yourself. Then extend the conversation.

> It would be really cool to work in an airport. What do you think?

10 **Discuss in pairs.** How does this strategy help you to communicate better? What are some other words or phrases you know that will help you learn more about the person you're talking to?

Go to p. 155.

16 **Before you read, think about this unit's topic.** You will read about two people. Predict what you'll learn about them.

17 **Learn new words.** Find these words in the reading. Look at each word's ending. Which of the words are professions? How do you know? Then listen and repeat. TR: 28

| advisor | to commute | to create | photographer | scientist |

18 **While you read, look for similarities and differences.** TR: 29

19 **After you read, work in pairs to answer the questions.**

1. What are Jimmy Chin's three jobs?

2. Jimmy enjoys traveling. How do you know this from the text?

3. Do you think a lot of people visit the places that Jimmy photographs? Why or why not?

4. Why does Kevin go to northern Alaska and the Arctic Sea?

5. Other than being a planetary scientist, what other job does Kevin have?

Adventures
Near and Far

These explorers love working in extreme places.

You're more likely to find photographer Jimmy Chin commuting to Mount Everest than to an office. Not only is he a photographer, he's also a professional climber and skier. He takes photographs and videos in some of the most amazing—but dangerous—places on Earth.

Jimmy has climbed and photographed the world's highest mountains in Nepal, Tibet, and Pakistan. And he does all of this while carrying heavy cameras. Why does Jimmy do such difficult work in such extreme places? "Creating films and photographs in situations that few others could experience is my life's inspiration," he says.

Jimmy isn't the only explorer working in extreme places. Planetary scientist Kevin Hand drills through the ice in northern Alaska and the Arctic Sea to study microscopic life in the water underneath it. He hopes that studying microscopic life under ice on Earth will help him to find and study life under the ice on Jupiter's moon Europa.

Not all of Kevin's work is in cold, faraway places, though. He also works with directors as a science advisor for movies, such as *Europa Report*. Kevin has even been in a movie! He was a featured scientist in the movie *Aliens of the Deep*.

Jimmy and Kevin make it clear that work doesn't have to be boring!

Jimmy Chin in Yosemite National Park, California, USA

20 **Work in pairs.** Compare and contrast Jimmy Chin and Kevin Hand.

21 **Discuss in groups.**

1. Jimmy and Kevin take risks doing their work. Would you want a job where you had to take risks? Do you think it's good or bad to take risks? Why?

2. Do you think it's important to explore outer space? Why or why not?

33

22 **Before you watch, discuss in pairs.**

1. Look at the photo. What do you think the divers are looking for? List three ideas.

2. Imagine you're diving in this fissure. Describe what you see.

23 **Work in pairs.** You're going to watch *Searching for Life in Iceland's Fissures*. In this video, you'll see scientists enter the water of an underground fissure in Iceland. Predict a problem they might have.

24 **Watch scene 2.1.** **While you watch, check your prediction from Activity 23.**

25 **After you watch, work in pairs.** Answer the questions below.

1. How did Jónína feel the first time she dove in a fissure? Why?

2. What were Jónína and her team the first to do?

3. Why is it risky to dive in the fissure?

4. Why does it seem that there isn't much living in the waters?

5. How do scientists get the material off the walls of the fissures?

6. What do the scientists do with the samples they collect underwater?

7. What are Jónína's two passions?

Jónína and a team member explore Iceland's underwater fissures.

26 **Work in pairs.** Both Jónína and Guillermo de Anda are underwater explorers. How are their jobs similar? How are they different? Write your ideas in a Venn diagram.

27 **Work in pairs.** In the video, Jónína says, "So far we made some exciting discoveries of species that no one knew existed in Iceland." Why is it important to discover new information about an animal species? Give an example of what can be learned from new discoveries.

28 **Choose an activity.**

1. **Work independently.** What things other than animals can we study underwater? List three things and give an example of what we could learn from each one.

2. **Work in pairs.** Research another job that combines diving and science. Imagine you have that job. Explain your job to the class.

3. **Work in groups.** Find out about a person from your country who recently discovered something unusual. Prepare a profile of this person. Present it to the class.

Possessives: Showing ownership

This **dentist's** job isn't done in an office.

Dr. Perkins's job is to get the equipment on the plane.

Pilots' days are very long.

My job is helping sick people. What's **your** job?

The flying dentist thinks **her** job is great. The pilot likes **his** job, too. The job also has **its** advantages.

At **our** job, we help everyone, no matter what **their** problem is.

29 **Read.** Circle the possessives.

My name is Dr. Smith, and I'm a flight dentist with the Royal Flying Doctor Service (RFDS) in Australia. Its 63 planes fly every day of the year. Our goal is to deliver health services to people in rural areas.

I work with a great team. Our days are very long, but no two days are ever the same. One doctor on the team says that he loves his job because it's never boring! I don't have an office so I check patients' teeth in their homes. This morning I checked Ms. Lee's teeth in her living room, and the Watson family's teeth on their porch!

30 **Work independently.** Interview classmates to learn about jobs that their family and friends have. Put an X over the job when you find a classmate who knows someone with that job. Play until you cross out five jobs. Then report to the class using possessives.

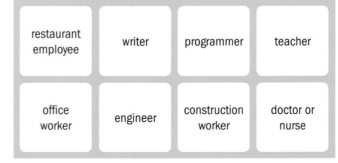

Is someone in your family an engineer?

Yes, my uncle is an engineer! He loves his job.

restaurant employee	writer	programmer	teacher
office worker	engineer	construction worker	doctor or nurse

A descriptive paragraph should include the following:

Title: Gives an idea of what the paragraph is about
Topic sentence: Is usually the first sentence; tells what the paragraph is about
Details: Give more information about the topic sentence
Concluding sentence: Ends the paragraph

31 **Read the model.** Work in pairs to identify the title, topic sentence, details, and concluding sentence. Underline each part.

A Typical Work Day

My aunt has a great job at an orangutan sanctuary. She's the daytime babysitter for a five-month-old orangutan named Coco. Coco's mother died, so they need to take care of her 24 hours a day. When my aunt arrives in the morning, she gives Coco milk in her bottle and changes her diaper. She does this several times a day. Then she works as her teacher, teaching her the skills she needs for living in the forest, such as climbing. Coco likes to climb up, but not down! She screams for my aunt's help sometimes. My aunt hugs her when she gets scared. In the early evening, it's Coco's bedtime and their time together that day is over. They put her to bed and go home. My aunt says, "I love Coco, and I love my job!"

32 **Work in pairs.** What is unusual about the orangutan babysitter's job? Would you like to have this job? Why or why not?

33 **Write.** Describe the daily routine of someone you know who has an unusual job. Include a title, a topic sentence, details, and a concluding sentence.

Do What You Love

"I have the coolest job in the world because I love what I do!"

—Guillermo de Anda
National Geographic Explorer, Underwater Archaeologist

1. **Watch scene 2.2.**

2. Guillermo loved diving from a very young age. How do you think this helped him to choose a career? How does he combine his love of diving with his love of science?

3. What career do you want to have? What will you need to do to prepare for this career? If you choose this career, will you be doing what you love? Explain.

Make an Impact

(A) **Write a want ad.**

- Imagine you own a company and you need someone for an unusual job.
- Create a want ad. Write a job description. Include information about your company.
- Share your want ad with the class. Is anybody interested in your unusual job? Interview them for the job!

(B) **Create a comic strip.**

- Interview a person who has a typical job. Ask this person to mention three or four unusual or unexpected parts of the job.
- Design a comic strip to illustrate the unusual aspects of this person's job.
- Share your comic strip with the class.

(C) **Plan a job fair for unusual jobs.**

- Find information about five interesting and unusual careers.
- Make posters showing a typical day for these workers.
- Display the posters in your classroom. Talk to your classmates about what each job involves.

Express Yourself

GoTravel
REVIEWS

GONDOLA TOURS OF VENICE

■ ■ ■ ■ ◻ **210 reviews**

■ ■ ■ ■ ■ — JGirl, Seoul

"Our gondolier saved my vacation!"

Well, I'm in Venice, Italy, with my family! Venice is incredible! The city is hundreds of years old, and it's built on WATER. People get around on special boats called *gondolas*, and today I had my first gondola ride!

A gondolier controls the gondola using an oar and his own strength. (These gondoliers are REALLY strong.) The gondolier's job is to describe Venice's culture and history as he takes you through the city's canals. Our gondolier was so good at telling stories I almost forgot I was sharing the ride with my parents.

That might sound exciting, and it was, but of course I was with . . . my dad. And Dad thought it would be funny to wear a striped shirt to match the gondolier's shirt. Can you say *embarrassing*?!

My parents loved looking at the beautiful bridges, churches, and palaces along the route. I really enjoyed listening to our gondolier talk about his work. He told us that it takes years of study and practice to get the job. Who knew? He also told us that of all the gondoliers in Venice, only one is a woman! I think I need to change that! It's time to start training for my dream job! Maybe my dad will let me borrow his shirt. ;)

Gondola Tours of Venice gave me a great tour of a beautiful city—and an interesting idea for my future career! I recommend the gondola tour to anyone who's interested in learning about unusual places and unusual jobs . . . especially if they're stuck on a boat with their parents!

Gondolas in Venice, Italy

2 **Work in groups.** Discuss the review.

1. Does JGirl's review make you want to visit Venice and go on a gondola ride? Why or why not?

2. Do you think the review gives enough information? Is it funny and interesting? What else would you like to know about Venice or about Gondola Tours of Venice?

3 **Connect ideas.** In Unit 1, you learned about exploring and unusual places. In Unit 2, you learned about unusual jobs. What connection do you see between the two units?

4 **Choose an activity.**

1. Choose a topic:
   • an unusual place
   • an unusual job

2. Choose a way to express yourself:
   • a review
   • an advertisement
   • an interview

3. Present your work.

41

Secrets of the Dark

"To me, science is fiction because sometimes it just seems unreal. Looking at bioluminescence, it's just beautiful. It's artwork."

—David Gruber

Blue ghost fireflies

1. In the photo, fireflies create a beautiful light. What other things in nature produce light?

2. Bioluminescent animals use lights to communicate with one another. How do humans use lights to communicate?

3. Where do you feel comfortable in the dark? Why?

1 **What would be difficult about living without sunlight for two months every year?** Discuss. Then listen and read. TR: 32

For most of us, the days are divided into day and night. But for two months each winter in northern Norway, it's **dark** for 20 hours a day. There is no **sunrise** or **sunset** because the sun never gets above the **horizon**.

Would you like to live in **darkness** for this long? It may seem difficult, but many Norwegians love the beautiful colors of these months. To the **south** are the red and gold colors of the horizon. To the **north**, the sky is a magnificent blue. Even the moon and stars look blue. In the towns, streetlights shine like little yellow diamonds.

People do need light to be healthy and happy. Since they don't have much daylight during this time of the year, Norwegians

In the town of Longyearbyen, in northern Norway, there's no sunlight from November to January. However, the sun doesn't set from the end of April to the end of August.

exercise and eat foods with vitamins A and D, nutrients people normally get from being in the sun. And darkness doesn't stop Norwegians from having a good time. Each winter, people are skiing on hills and skating on ponds that are **lit up**. Some people are dogsledding (with **headlights**, of course!). Others are going to film and music **festivals**. And other people are spending time with friends in cafés and restaurants. Of course, not everyone is so **active** in the dark months. Many people are just **going to sleep** a little earlier until the sun returns in the spring.

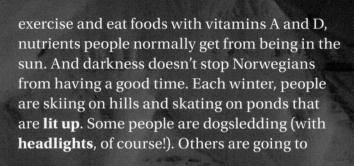

2 **Learn new words.** Listen and repeat. TR: 33

3 **Work in pairs.** What would you like about living in the dark for two months? What wouldn't you like? Write three things for each. Compare your list with your partner's.

17 **Before you read, discuss in pairs.** What do you know about the ocean and life in the ocean? What do you want to learn?

18 **Look at the text and photos quickly.** Then answer the questions.

1. Who is this reading about?
2. What sea animal has really big eyes?

19 **Learn new words.** Find the words in the text. Guess their meaning. Then look at the first meaning given for each word in the dictionary. Compare those meanings with your guesses. Then listen and repeat. TR: 42

| dawn | to fascinate | to glow | to observe | pattern |

20 **While you read, think about what makes animals in the deep ocean different.** TR: 43

21 **After you read, work in pairs.** Check *T* for true or *F* for false.

1. David observes life in the ocean when it's dark. Ⓣ Ⓕ

2. We know a lot about everything that lives in the ocean. Ⓣ Ⓕ

3. We can see all the glowing colors in the ocean with our eyes. Ⓣ Ⓕ

4. Only one type of animal glows in the dark through the lens of David's camera. Ⓣ Ⓕ

5. A lot of animals at the bottom of the ocean make their own light. Ⓣ Ⓕ

6. The vampire squid has very large eyes to help it see in the dark. Ⓣ Ⓕ

22 **Review.** Look at your answers from Activity 18. Were they correct? What else did you learn about the person and the sea animal?

50

IN THE
DARK
OF THE
OCEAN

A shark glows bright green through the filters of David's camera.

here are incredible creatures living in
he darkness.

In the darkness before dawn, marine
iologist David Gruber dives into the ocean to
bserve the amazing creatures that live there.
Seventy-one percent of Earth is ocean, and
much of it is dark, with tons of life down there
hat we don't know about," he says.

David discovered that many sea animals
an see colors in the water that we cannot. So
e designed a camera that allows him to see
he colors just as a fish does. His camera shows
secret world of neon green, red, and orange
olors on ocean life that glows in the dark.

In this fascinating world, David discovered
special kind of shark that glows bright with
reen spots. "When you see all these little
right spots and patterns, it's like flowers and
utterflies. Why do they make patterns?
t's to attract each other. It's to recognize each
ther," he says.

At the bottom of the ocean where there is
o light at all, many animals produce their
wn light. The unusual vampire squid is an
xample. It can turn itself on or off, just like
lamp. It also has very big eyes to help it see
n the dark. In fact, compared to its body
ize, the vampire squid has the largest eyes of
ny animal in the world. And this is just one

animal: ninety percent of the animals tha
at the bottom of the ocean produce their c
light.

It's easy to see why the darkness of the
fascinates David. "Marine animals in the
ocean produce lights to communicate wit
each other," says David. "It's an underwate
disco party. We human beings are the last
to join in!"

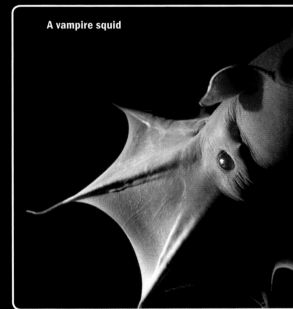
A vampire squid

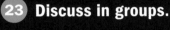

23 **Discuss in groups.**

1. What things about the oc
   fascinate you? Why do the
   fascinate you?

2. It's difficult to study the
   ocean at night because of
   the darkness. What are s
   other difficulties David m
   have when studying the
   ocean at night?

3. Do you think it's importa
   learn about what lives in

VIDEO ▶

24 **Before you watch, discuss in pairs.**

1. What did you love doing as a small child? Do you still love it? What else do you love doing now?

2. Are you interested in learning about what's in the ocean? Why or why not?

25 **Work in pairs.** The title of the video you're going to watch is *What Glows Beneath*. Think of what you have learned about David Gruber and his work. Then make two lists: *What I have learned about David* and *What I want to learn about David*.

26 Watch scene 3.1. **While you watch, circle the correct answers.**

1. David first became fascinated by the ocean by *surfing / scuba diving.*

2. David wondered *if it would be hard to study biology / what was beneath him in the water.*

3. David wanted to photograph the ocean so that he can *sell his photos to magazines / understand how fish see it.*

4. David says that *there's still a lot to learn about / scientists have discovered all of the species of* the ocean.

5. According to David, the future of exploration is finding out *why humans don't glow / how humans fit in among nature.*

27 **After you watch, work in pairs to answer the questions.**

1. What was David's hobby when he was a teenager?
2. How does this hobby connect to his job?
3. What is special about how David studies the ocean?
4. What do the filters in David's camera allow him to do?

28 **Work in pairs.** List three of the sea animals you saw in the video. Describe what they look like. Now think of three sea animals you know about or have seen photos of. How are they different from the animals in the video?

David uses a camera with special filters to explore the dark ocean.

29 **Choose an activity.**

1. **Work independently.** Imagine that you went scuba diving and saw some of the animals in the video. Write a postcard to a friend or family member, describing what you saw. In your postcard, explain how you were able to see the animals glow.

2. **Work in pairs.** Role-play a conversation between David and a reporter who's asking him about his work. Share your dialogue with the class.

3. **Work in groups.** Prepare a glow-in-the-dark presentation. Each person finds out about a different sea animal that glows in the dark. Draw it or find a photo of it. Write three pieces of information about it. Present your group of animals to the class.

Understand and Protect

"People want to protect things they love and understand. The more I can share about the amazing animals I get to explore, the more people may want to help protect them."

—David Gruber
National Geographic Explorer, Marine Biologist

1. Watch scene 3.2.

2. David cares deeply about the ocean and ocean life. Why is it important to protect animals in the ocean? How does David's work help protect them?

3. What do you want to protect? Why? How can you get others to care about this?

Make an Impact

A **Design a poster.**

· Research animals or plants that glow in the dark. Find out how and why they glow.

· Make a poster to describe three of the glow-in-the-dark organisms you researched. Include photos.

· Present your poster to the class.

B **Write a blog entry.**

· Research a place that is light for more than two months a year.

· Pretend that you visit during the light season. Write a blog about your visit. Include photos.

· Publish your blog. Answer questions and respond to your classmates' comments.

C **Make a "day-and-night" video.**

· Choose an interesting place in your region.

· Make a video of that place during the day and during the night. Mention what is the same and what is different.

· Share your video with the class.

**Bioluminescent fungi glowing
on a tree trunk**

Living Together

"Let's think about what we can do today to make sure our grandchildren have the option of seeing wildlife in the future."

—Amy Dickman

A rhinoceros and its caretaker at a conservancy in Kenya

1. What's happening in the photo? How do you think the man feels? The animal?

2. What are situations where people and animals live together peacefully? What are situations where they don't get along?

3. Do you think that seeing wild animals where they live is a good idea? Why or why not?

1 **Why might baboons and humans come into contact with each other?** Discuss. Then listen and read. TR: 45

Human-**wildlife conflict** is a big problem all over the world today, and it's getting bigger. Imagine coming home and finding a baboon or two eating breakfast at your table! That would definitely be a conflict between a human, you, and wildlife, the baboons! Because baboons are **wild**, this type of conflict could be dangerous.

In Cape Town, South Africa, humans are **interacting** with baboons more than ever, right in their own neighborhoods. Because about half of the natural baboon **habitat** and food in this region **disappeared**, baboons needed to find new ways to get food. So they started going into urban areas and stealing the food they need for survival.

A family of baboons at the breakfast table

Baboons are very **smart** animals. Once they **learn** that they can easily get food from humans, they won't try as hard to hunt for their own food. People who live near baboon habitats have to control this **behavior** by limiting the baboons' **access** to human food and garbage.

Both humans and wildlife **need** protection from each other. Luckily, in some places in South Africa, there are people who work as baboon monitors. Their job is to keep baboons away from homes. Because baboons are **afraid of** loud noises, monitors use noise-making devices to **frighten** them away. They might also use paintballs to frighten the baboons.

The monitors don't form relationships with the baboons, but they don't mistreat them, either. They simply work to limit conflicts between humans and wildlife.

2 **Learn new words.** Listen and repeat. TR: 46

3 **Work in pairs.** Think about a time when an unwanted animal came into your house. How did you feel? What did you do?

Amy Dickman is trying to solve *wildlife / conflicts* between humans and the *wild / interacting* big cats in villages around Ruaha National Park in Tanzania. The big cat *habitat / behavior* in the park is disappearing. As a result, these big cats *frighten / need* to find new ways to get food. So they go onto farms and kill farm animals for food. Because the farmers are *smart / afraid of* losing their animals, they kill the big cats.

Amy is trying to change the *wildlife / behavior* of villagers toward the big cats. She's also helping villagers find better ways to protect their animals. Amy believes that people should *interact / disappear* with wildlife in ways that give both groups *habitat / access* to the resources they need.

Learn new words. Listen for these words and complete the sentences. Then listen and repeat. TR: 47 and 48

to hunt	to mistreat	relationship	survival

1. Wild animals _____ for their food.
2. Dogs and their owners have a special _____ .
3. All living things need food and water for their _____ .
4. People who hit animals _____ them.

Choose an activity. Work in pairs.

1. Discuss. What animals in your country are losing their habitat? What problems do they have? What are people doing about it?

2. Make a list of three reasons why people hunt wild animals. Do you think humans should change their behavior so that they don't need to hunt?

3. Find a group where you live that works with wild animals. Learn about what they do and why they do it.

Asking for reasons	Giving reasons
Why <u>are villagers afraid of wild animals</u>?	Because <u>they're dangerous</u>.
<u>Farmers need to protect their animals from wild animals</u>. Do you know why?	It's because <u>wild animals hunt farm animals for food</u>.
<u>Wild animals are interacting with people more often</u>. Why is that?	Since <u>their habitats are disappearing, they're going where humans live</u>.

7 **Listen.** How do the speakers ask for and give reasons? Write the words and phrases you hear. **TR: 50**

8 **Read and complete the dialogue.**

Abdul: Look at this picture of people on an Indian tiger reserve.

Anna: The people are wearing masks. _____

Abdul: _____ they're trying to trick the tigers.

Anna: They're wearing the masks on the *backs* of their heads!

_____

Abdul: _____ tigers attack people from behind, they see the mask and think the person is looking at them. That scares them.

Anna: Incredible! But _____ do people go onto the tiger reserve?

Abdul: _____ they fish there. They also collect honey and wood in the reserves.

Anna: So the people wear masks _____ they believe the masks will protect them from tigers?

Abdul: That's right. In three years, tigers only attacked people who weren't wearing masks!

Anna: Wow! Tigers are smart, though. They might soon learn that people are tricking them.

9 **Work in pairs.** Take a card and read the sentence. Ask your partner for the reason. Your partner will answer the question. Then switch roles.

10 **Work in pairs.** Talk about animals. Tell about three problems, interesting facts, or interactions. Your partner will ask for reasons. Respond and then switch roles.

Why are there baboon monitors in Cape Town?

Baboons go into urban areas. Monitors help to keep them away from humans.

There are baboon monitors in Cape Town.

Go to p. 161.

63

Modals: Describing obligation and advice

Necessary	We **must** learn more about the fight to save rhinos.
	We **have to** protect rhinos.
Not necessary	We **don't have to** use products made from rhinoceros horn.
Recommended	We **shouldn't** ignore the rhino problem.
	Everyone **should** do something, even if it's a small action.

RHINOCEROS POPULATIONS WORLDWIDE

20,405 WHITE RHINO

5,055 BLACK RHINO

3,333 GREATER ONE-HORNED RHINO

<100 SUMATRAN RHINO

58–60 JAVAN RHINO

11 **Listen.** How can we save rhinos? Complete the sentences. Then check the correct box. TR: 52

	necessary	not necessary	recommended
1. Rangers _____ go into the rhino areas and catch the hunters.	☐	☐	☐
2. Rhino monitors _____ know when rhino babies are born.	☐	☐	☐
3. We _____ use rhino horn in medicine.	☐	☐	☐
4. We _____ keep some rhinos in protected places when they have their babies.	☐	☐	☐
5. We _____ tell people what to do to save rhinos.	☐	☐	☐

12 **Work in pairs.** Listen again to the passage. Write two additional ways to save rhinos. Say if they are *necessary*, *not necessary*, or *recommended*. TR: 53

1. _____

2. _____

13 **Work in pairs.** Give advice on how people can protect wildlife. Use *must*, *(don't) have to*, *should*, and *shouldn't*.

> We shouldn't hunt wild animals just for fun.

> You're right. And we must stop hunters that hunt for fur.

14 **Learn new words.** Listen to learn about saving sea turtles. Then listen and repeat.

TR: 54 and 55

Saving
Sea Turtles

Humans are sea turtles' biggest **predator**.

Sea turtle eggs are **prey** for seagulls as well as humans.

Sea turtles cannot **defend** themselves against humans.

The Turtle Hospital in Florida, USA, **rescues injured** sea turtles.

Sea turtles have to survive. We must all do something to help them.

15 **Work independently.** Think of another wild animal that is endangered. Write about why it's endangered. Give advice on how to protect it. Remember to use *must*, *(don't) have to*, *should*, and *shouldn't*.

_____

_____

_____

_____

16 **Work in groups.** Imagine you work for a group that helps protect sea turtles. What five pieces of advice would you give people on what to do?

> We must help people who sell eggs find other ways to make money.

17 **Before you read, discuss in pairs.** What does it mean to be an animal hero? What do you want to learn about the animal heroes?

18 **Learn new words.** Find these words in the text. Look for words that appear together, such as *domestic animals*. Then listen and repeat. TR: 56

to avoid	chemical	domestic	feeling	to sniff

19 **While you read, look for problems and solutions.** TR: 57

20 **After you read, work in pairs to answer the questions.**

1. What is Bart Weetjen's organization? What does it do?
2. Why does Bart think that rats are heroes?
3. How do landmines make life hard for farmers and villagers?
4. What lifesaving skill do dogs have?
5. What is one thing that rats and dogs both can do?

FOUR-LEGGED
Heroes

Animals with Amazing Abilities

Most people have mixed feelings about rats and avoid them if they can. Bart Weetjens thinks that we must treat rats as heroes.

Bart started an organization called APOPO in Tanzania. Bart's organization trains African giant pouched rats to sniff the ground in order to find underground landmines left in the area during past wars. Many of these landmines are still active. They often explode, killing and injuring thousands of people each year. Villagers avoid places where the dangerous landmines are. But much of this land could be used as valuable farmland if the mines weren't there. These rats are helping villagers get their land back.

The giant rats are never mistreated. None of them die doing their work. They even have sunblock put on their ears and tails while they work. And when they find a landmine, they get a treat!

While rats aren't usually seen as heroes, some domestic animals, like dogs, often are. There are many stories about dogs that save lives, but dogs have another lifesaving skill that we're still learning about. Just like landmine-sniffing rats, dogs have an amazing sense of smell. They're now being trained to sniff out chemicals from the body that are connected to certain diseases, sometimes even before doctors or laboratory tests can find them!

So the next time you see a rat or dog, don't be afraid. Remember, these animal heroes can save lives.

A medical dog sniffing for diseases

A giant pouched rat sniffing a landmine

21 **Complete the chart.** Write two problems and two solutions.

Problem	Solution

22 **Discuss in groups.**

1. Did the reading change your feelings about rats? Dogs? Explain.

2. What other animals do you know about that have helped people or saved lives? How did they help?

3. Imagine you train animals to help people or save lives. What kind of animal would you train? Why? How would it help?

67

23 **Before you watch, discuss in pairs.**

1. An orphan elephant is a young elephant that has no mother. What do you think happened to the orphans' mothers? Give one or two ideas.

2. Why do you think people have to take care of the young orphan elephants?

24 **Read and circle.** You're going to watch *The Elephant Whisperers.* Use the title to predict what the video is about. Circle the number.

1. Baby elephants in a zoo

2. Elephant and human conflicts

3. People who take care of baby elephants

25 Watch scene 4.1. **While you watch, write two words that describe the elephants and two words that describe the humans.**

Elephants:

_____

_____

Humans:

_____

_____

26 **Work in pairs.** Put the daily events in order, according to the video.

_____ The keepers feed and play with the elephants.

_____ The keepers and elephants go back to the camp.

_____ The keepers and elephants go to the bush.

___1___ The elephant keepers get up at 5:30 a.m.

_____ The elephants and their keepers go to bed.

27 **After you watch, read the sentences.** Decide if they are *true* or *false*. Check the correct answers.

1. The elephants are not very friendly. **T** **F**

2. The elephants are from different places in Kenya. **T** **F**

3. The elephants want to be alone. **T** **F**

4. The elephants only like to be with their keepers. **T** **F**

5. The keepers stay with the elephants at night so that they don't cry. **T** **F**

28 **Discuss in pairs.**

1. How are elephants and humans alike? Name three similarities.

2. What do you think is fun about being an elephant keeper? What do you think is hard?

29 **Choose an activity.**

1. **Work independently.** Imagine you're an elephant keeper. Write a letter to your family explaining a day in your life.

2. **Work in pairs.** Write a job advertisement for an elephant keeper. Describe the job and the type of person needed to do it.

3. **Work in groups.** In the video, you saw workers playing ball with the elephants. Think of at least three other fun ways that humans can interact with elephants. Present your ideas to the class.

Modals: Describing ability in present and past

Many types of wildlife today **can't** cross highways safely.

What **can** we do about it?

We **can** help them by building animal crossings.

In 1987, salamanders **couldn't** safely cross a street in Amherst, Massachusetts, USA.

How **could** they avoid cars?

People built tunnels under the street. This way, the salamanders **could** cross safely.

30 **Read.** Complete the paragraph with *can*, *can't*, *could*, or *couldn't*.

Highways _____ be dangerous for both humans and wildlife. Highways go though wildlife habitat, so animals _____ cross safely. When cars hit animals, people _____ get hurt, too.

This is changing now in many countries. Before 2011, elephants _____ safely cross a highway in Kenya. But now they _____ because the government built a tunnel under the highway.

On Christmas Island in Australia, cars killed around 500,000 red crabs every year. People thought of ways they _____ help the crabs. They built special bridges over the road. Now the crabs _____ be harmed because they _____ climb over the bridges to safety.

In Holland, people knew they _____ help their wildlife stay alive. So they worked to create over 600 animal crossings. Now wildlife and people _____ travel where they need to go safely.

31 **Work in pairs.** Play Tic-Tac-Talk. Describe your own abilities now and in the past. Mark X or O. Try to get three in a row.

> When I was six, I couldn't teach my dog to do tricks.

can	coun't	could
could	WILD	can't
couldn't	can	can't

70

Go to p. 159.

After you write, reread your paragraph. Make sure it's organized and clear. When you have a good draft, proofread your paragraph. Make note of spelling, grammar, and punctuation mistakes. Then rewrite the paragraph, correcting the mistakes.

32 **Read the model.** Underline the spelling mistakes in the paragraph. Circle the grammar mistakes.

Wong Siew Te at the Bornean Sun Bear Conservation Centre in Malaysia felt both sad and happy the day he take Natalie, a sun bear, back to her natural home in the forrest. Hunters killed Natalie's mother when she was a baby, so she couldn't do everything bears need for servivel in a forest. Te took care of her for almost five years. He cared for her like a duaghter. He teached Natalie how to live like a wild bear. For example, he teached her how to find food and build nests. Te knew he can't keep Natalie at the reserve forever because sun bears belong in the forest. When she was. ready, he set her free in the forest. Today he could uses his computer to check on Natalie in her new home. He can do this because she has a specal collar that lets him know where she is. Te and his team is proud they could help Natalie survive in her habitat.

33 **Discuss in pairs.** Do you always read your paragraphs after writing them? What mistakes do you most often make in your writing? How can proofreading help you to become a better writer?

34 **Write.** Write about a special relationship between an animal and a human. Then proofread your paragraph and correct the mistakes.

Start Small

"If everyone did something small, it would be huge."

—Amy Dickman
National Geographic Explorer, Animal Conservationist

1. **Watch scene 4.2.**

2. What do you think is the most important thing Amy is doing to help big cats? How does Amy's work help both humans and wildlife?

3. What are some simple things you could do to help protect wildlife? How could it help both humans and animals?

Make an Impact

Ⓐ Raise awareness for an endangered animal.

- Research an unusual wild animal that is endangered.
- Make posters or brochures with information about that animal.
- Share the information with your classmates.

Ⓑ Teach others about a human-wildlife conflict.

- Research a human-wildlife conflict where you live.
- Find out what's being done to solve this issue.
- Make a presentation to your class.

Ⓒ Create a video interview.

- Role-play an interview between a wild-animal expert and a journalist.
- Talk about the wild animal and the problems it faces.
- Film your interview and share it with the class.

Orphaned koalas with a caregiver in Queensland, Australia

Express Yourself

1 Read and listen to the story about Amy Dickman and a lion. TR: 59

SLEEPING WITH A LION

AMY'S FIRST NIGHT IN THE WILD OF TANZANIA WAS THE SCARIEST NIGHT OF HER LIFE.

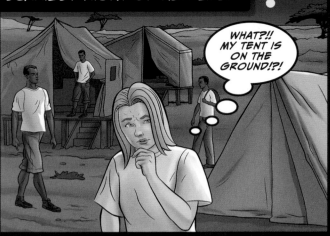

WHAT?!! MY TENT IS ON THE GROUND!?!

AMY WAS EXCITED TO BE IN AFRICA. BUT THEN SHE HEARD LIONS CALLING IN THE DARK NIGHT.

I MUST BE BRAVE!

A LION WAS WALKING AROUND AND SNIFFING HER TENT! AMY WAS AFRAID IT MIGHT ATTACK HER!

GRRR!

WHAT SHOULD I DO?!?

2 **Work in groups.** Discuss the story.

1. How did Amy's story make you feel? Explain.

2. What would you do in Amy's situation?

3. What other problems do people who work with wildlife have?

3 **Connect ideas.**

Discuss the story. In Unit 3, you learned about what humans and animals do at night. In Unit 4, you learned about human and animal interaction. What connection do you see between the two units?

THE LION LAY DOWN ON AMY'S ARM. IT FELL ASLEEP! AMY WAS VERY FRIGHTENED.

OH, NO! I CAN'T MOVE MY ARM!

AMY COULD FEEL THE HEAT FROM THE LION'S BODY. HER TENT BECAME VERY, VERY HOT. SHE COULD HARDLY BREATHE! SHE WAS VERY SCARED. FINALLY SHE FELL ASLEEP TOO.

IN THE MORNING, THE LION WAS GONE. THERE WERE PAW PRINTS ALL AROUND HER TENT.

WAS IT A DREAM?

4 **Choose an activity.**

1. Choose a topic:
   - the world at night
   - human and animal interaction

2. Choose a way to express yourself:
   - an oral story
   - a comic strip
   - a play

3. Present your work.

75

What We Wear

"The right clothes can make life a lot easier and, in some cases, even save your life."

A man in a protective suit, ready to explore the Darvaza Crater, Turkmenistan

1. Describe the clothes you see in the photo. Do you think these clothes are important at this place? Why or why not?

2. What do you wear to school? On special days? On weekends?

3. What did you buy the last time you went shopping for clothing and accessories? Why did you buy these things?

1 What clothes do you like to wear?

Discuss. Then listen and read. TR: 60

At some point, you've probably looked at old photos of people and asked yourself, "Why did they **wear** *that*? What were they *thinking*?" The people in the photo probably thought that they **looked** great! The truth is, nothing stays the same forever, especially in the world of **fashion**. What's cool today will be ugly before long. What we like to wear changes all the time.

A **century** ago, many men—from businessmen to taxi drivers—wore **suits** to work. Even young boys regularly wore suits and **ties**. Women didn't just wear skirts or dresses when they wanted to **dress up**. They wore them all the time—even if they were just staying home!

Over time, **casual** clothes replaced **formal** clothes. For example, **jeans** are very popular today. They were first made for workers who needed pants with strong fabric that didn't tear easily. In 1873, tailor Jacob Davis and businessman Levi Strauss created denim pants they called *overalls* because people wore them over their clothes. Cowboys wore denim jeans and, thanks to the Western movies of the 1930s, many people began wearing them. Today, jeans and a **sweatshirt** are practically a **uniform** for teens around the world.

Cowboys helped make jeans popular.

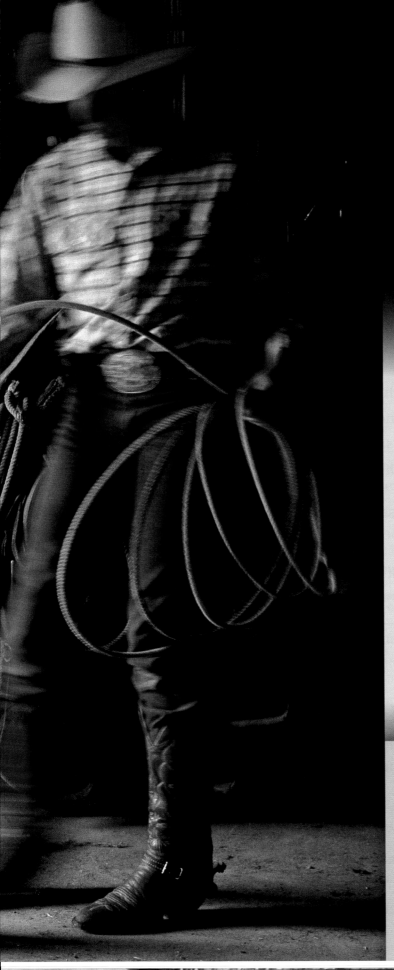

Louis XIV of France

Like clothes, shoes have also changed over time. You may prefer to wear sneakers, but in the past both men and women wore shoes with high **heels**. In the early eighteenth century, King Louis XIV of France started wearing tights with red high-heeled shoes. This was the fashion for nearly a century before men began wearing more **practical** shoes without heels.

Things change. You might think your clothes are fashionable now, but if a hundred years from now people see a photo of you, they might just ask, "Why did they wear *that*?"

2 **Learn new words.** Listen and repeat.
TR: 61

3 **Work in pairs.** Think about photos that you've seen of people from long ago. Compare their clothes with what you wear now.

79

21 **Before you watch, discuss in pairs.** Imagine you're going to work in the desert for one full day. What clothes should you wear? Why? What other things should you bring with you? Make a list.

22 **Work in pairs.** In the video, you will hear about a problem the explorer Andrés Ruzo had while working in the desert. Look at the photo. What do you think the problem might be?

23 Watch scene 5.1. **While you watch, circle the words you hear.**

boots	comfortable	cool	fashion
heels	practical	protect	shirt
shoes	suit	sweatshirt	warm

24 **After you watch, work in pairs to answer the questions.**

1. What are the soles of boat shoes made like?

2. How are boat shoes practical?

3. What kind of environments does Andrés work in?

4. Why is the right clothing important for him?

5. What did he and his team bring for protection from the sun?

6. How did the team use the item for protection?

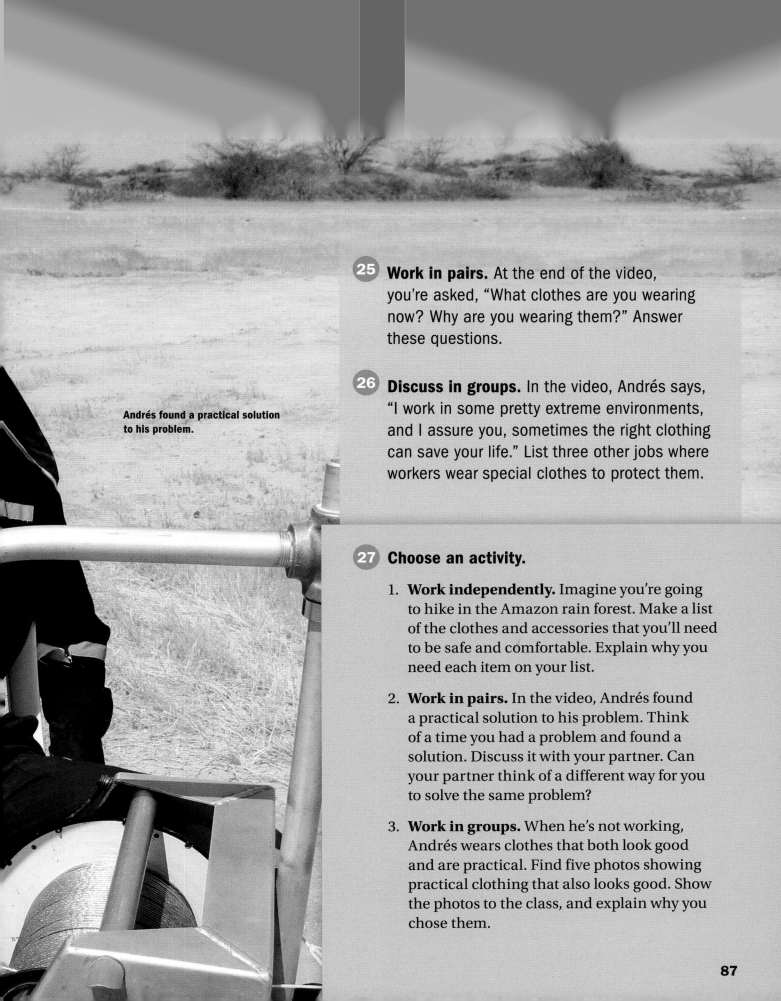

Andrés found a practical solution to his problem.

25 **Work in pairs.** At the end of the video, you're asked, "What clothes are you wearing now? Why are you wearing them?" Answer these questions.

26 **Discuss in groups.** In the video, Andrés says, "I work in some pretty extreme environments, and I assure you, sometimes the right clothing can save your life." List three other jobs where workers wear special clothes to protect them.

27 **Choose an activity.**

1. **Work independently.** Imagine you're going to hike in the Amazon rain forest. Make a list of the clothes and accessories that you'll need to be safe and comfortable. Explain why you need each item on your list.

2. **Work in pairs.** In the video, Andrés found a practical solution to his problem. Think of a time you had a problem and found a solution. Discuss it with your partner. Can your partner think of a different way for you to solve the same problem?

3. **Work in groups.** When he's not working, Andrés wears clothes that both look good and are practical. Find five photos showing practical clothing that also looks good. Show the photos to the class, and explain why you chose them.

Simple past: Saying what happened

Long ago the plague **made** people very sick.

Doctors **had** to help people with the plague.

Doctors **wore** special protective suits. This way they **didn't** get sick.

Doctors also **put** on red eyeglasses. They **thought** the color red would protect them.

28 **Read.** Complete the sentences with the simple past form of the verbs in parentheses. For help, go to p. 148.

Doctors _____ (begin) wearing protective suits in England in the mid-1300s. They _____ (think) these suits _____ (keep) them safe from a sickness called the *plague*. So they _____ (wear) birdlike masks and long leather coats. The coats _____ (go) all the way

A protective suit

to the ground. Doctors always _____ (bring) a cane to their patients' houses. That way, they _____ (not have) to use their hands to touch the patient.

In the 1940s, people _____ (make) a new kind of protective suit. The suit _____ (not leave) any part of the body uncovered. The rubber fabric _____ (give) people good protection. People _____ (get) into the suit from the front. Then they _____ (put) on long gloves, boots, and a hood. The suit _____ (have) a special machine to help them breathe.

29 **Work in pairs.** Toss the cube. Ask a question about the past using the words on the cube. Your partner answers the question.

What did you wear to the concert?

I wore a blue dress with black shoes.

Go to p. 173.

what / wear

how / make

who / see

WRITING

The last step in writing is publishing. After you write, review, and proofread your work, you're ready to publish. When you publish, you let other people read your work.

30 **Read the model.** Do you think this essay is ready to be published? Why or why not? Discuss in pairs.

Before 1870, there were no soccer uniforms. Players wore their own clothes, which made it hard to know which team they were on. The first soccer uniform had long, loose shorts. Players wore striped, formal shirts with collars and buttons. The entire uniform was made of a heavy fabric, such as wool. Players then put on leather soccer boots that went up over their ankles.

Soccer uniforms have changed many times through the years. Today, soccer uniforms are very different. The shorts are shorter, and the whole uniform is made out of light fabric. This keeps soccer players cool as they run. Instead of boots, soccer players wear soft leather shoes. Each team now has its own colors. For example, players on the Brazilian soccer team wear bright yellow and green shirts, blue shorts, and white socks. But these uniforms will change, too. After all, sports teams need uniforms that are practical but also in fashion!

English soccer players wearing uniforms, 1888

31 **Discuss in pairs.** Who do you think would find this essay interesting? Where should the author publish this essay?

32 **Write.** Research another uniform that has changed over time. Write an essay about the changes. Proofread your work. Then publish it by sharing it with your classmates.

Learn to Adapt

"Adaptation is key to survival. Whether it's wearing a coat on a cold day or finding new sources of green energy—our ability to adapt to life's challenges allows us to thrive."

—Andrés Ruzo
National Geographic Explorer, Geoscientist

1. **Watch scene 5.2.**

2. How does the environment you're in affect your clothing choices? Give examples.

3. Andrés says it's important to adapt, or change our behavior, to respond to what's happening around us. Give examples of a time when you did this, and a time when you didn't. What happened in each situation?

Make an Impact

A **Be a clothing designer.**

· Design an accessory or article of clothing that will look good and protect you.

· Draw a picture of it. Write an explanation to tell why it looks good and is practical.

· Present your design to the class.

B **Plan and conduct a clothing scavenger hunt.**

· As a group, prepare a list of clothing items and accessories.

· Look around your home, your school, or local clothing stores. Take photos of the most interesting examples of each of the items on your list.

· Create a photo gallery to share your group's best photos. Describe the items and why you liked them.

C **Prepare a history presentation.**

· Research an article of clothing or accessory not presented in this unit. Find out how it has changed over the years.

· Create a poster or computer presentation about the item you chose. Use photos to show how the item has changed.

· Share your presentation with the class.

Mix and Mash

"Different is okay."
—Josh Ponte

Sea is for Cookie, a mash-up created from *The Great Wave off Kanagawa* and a television character called Cookie Monster

1. What are the different parts of this image?

2. What do you think of this image?

3. Think of two things that you could put together to make something different and new. What are they? What can you make?

93

1 **What types of music do you like?**
Discuss. Then listen and repeat. TR: 74

Mixing different styles of music creates a unique sound called a *mash-up*. Musicians have been creating mash-ups for more than fifty years. Many combine sounds from just two **songs**, but some might **include** parts from as many as twenty-five songs!

Many mash-up artists are **DJs** who use electronic equipment to mix together songs that already exist. These DJs decide what songs to use and how to mix them. Then they **record** their mash-ups. Next the DJs **edit** their **recordings** to make sure they sound as **cool** as possible.

DJs aren't the only ones that create musical mash-ups: bands do, too. One band that does this is the WagakkiBand from Japan. This band mixes the sounds of **traditional** Japanese instruments with rock music. The song they **performed** in their first **video** was a big hit. More than 30 million people saw the video on the Internet. People from all over the world downloaded the song from this video.

Another mash-up band is Gokh-Bi System from Dakar, Senegal. This band mixes rap with ancient West African music in a style called "ancient-meets-urban." The band performs with other famous singers and artists. **Fans** come from all over to hear them play.

People have different **opinions** of mash-up music. Some people prefer more traditional music styles. Others think that a mix of sounds is cooler than just one type of music. But no matter what you think of them, mash-ups provide an **audio** experience you won't forget!

2 **Learn new words.** Listen and repeat.
TR: 75

3 **Work in pairs.** Why do you think some musicians mix modern and traditional music? Do you think it's a good idea to do this? Why or why not?

WagakkiBand with traditional and modern instruments

A Feast
FOR THE
Eyes

Using food to create art

We've all seen art created from paint, clay, metal, and stone. But British photographer and artist Carl Warner goes to the supermarket to buy his art supplies. Carl creates what he calls *foodscapes*. He combines different types of food to imitate real landscapes. Then he photographs them. One of his foodscapes, *Carts and Balloons*, is a countryside scene. In this foodscape a few leafy green stalks of broccoli are a forest. A few pieces of

---

17 **Before you read, discuss in pairs.** Describe the most unusual piece of art you've seen. What did you like about it? What didn't you like about it?

18 **Learn new words.** Find these words in the reading. What do you think they mean? Notice examples that give their meaning. Then listen and repeat. TR: 84

| to imagine | to imitate | modern | original | weird |

19 **While you read, try to visualize, or see a picture in your mind, the artwork being described.** TR: 85

20 **After you read, work in pairs to answer the questions.**

1. What's a foodscape?
2. How did Carl create the landscape you see above?
3. Why does Carl create foodscapes?
4. Who asked Giuseppe Arcimboldo to paint his portrait?
5. Why did Giuseppe call the portrait *Vertumnus*?

Celery Island by Carl Warner

bread are used to make a cart. There are some berries in the cart and some potatoes as rocks. A few yellow corncobs and cucumbers are the fields. Hot-air balloons, made from bunches of bananas and other fruit, float in the sky. Some clouds of white bread float in the sky, too. It might seem a little weird to create art out of food, but Carl hopes that his work will get children excited about eating healthy foods.

Combining food and art is not a modern idea. Giuseppe Arcimboldo, a sixteenth-century Italian painter, also combined different types of food to create original art. In 1590 the Roman Emperor Rudolf II asked Giuseppe to paint his portrait. The result was really unusual! Called *Vertumnus*, after the Roman god of fruit, the painting shows a face made of fruit, vegetables, and flowers. Giuseppe painted one pea pod for each top eyelid, two baby onions for each bottom eyelid, one grape for each eye, a pear for the nose, an apple for one cheek and a peach for the other. Can you imagine what the emperor's face looked like? Luckily the emperor was happy with this unusual portrait!

21 **Work in pairs.** You read about two pieces of food art in the reading: the foodscape *Carts and Balloons* and the portrait *Vertumnus*. Choose one of the pieces to draw. Draw your pictures individually, and then compare your work. How are they similar? How are they different?

22 **Discuss in groups.**

1. Imagine you're creating a piece of food art. What picture do you make? What foods do you use to make it?

2. What problems do you think food artists have when they work? Name two or three.

3. Imagine you're an artist. What everyday things (other than food) could you use to create art? What would you create with those things?

4. Do you think combining food and art is a good idea? Why or why not?

23 **Before you watch, discuss in pairs.**

1. DJs mix music to create new songs. Why do you think they do this?
2. Choose two songs you both like. What part would you choose from each song to create your mash-up? What would your mash-up song be called?

24 **Write.** You're going to watch *What's in a Mash-Up?* Use what you've learned in the unit so far to answer that question.

_____

_____

25 **Watch scene 6.1. While you watch, circle the types of mash-ups mentioned in the video.**

animal	art	book	fashion
food	music	mythical	sport

26 **After you watch, work in pairs to answer the questions.**

1. How long have people been creating mash-ups?
2. What is the Great Sphinx of Giza a mash-up of?
3. What mythical creature is a mash-up of a man and a horse?
4. What two sports combine to make up *volenis*?
5. What is another name for *food mash-up*?
6. How is a ramen burger different from a regular hamburger?

A DJ can create a mash-up by mixing music.

27 **Work in pairs.** Of all the mash-ups you've learned about so far, which is the most interesting? The least interesting? Explain your answers.

28 **Discuss in groups.**

1. At the end of the video, you're asked, "What would you mash up?" Discuss your answers to this question.

2. Give another example of a mash-up from history. Describe it and its individual parts.

3. What do you think might be difficult in creating a mash-up? Consider art, food, and music mash-ups in your answer.

29 **Choose an activity.**

1. **Work independently.** Imagine you're a centaur. How does it help you? What's difficult about it? Write a paragraph to explain.

2. **Work in pairs.** Think of a mash-up you know. Create an advertisement for it. Describe what it's made of and what's special about it. Present your ad to the class.

3. **Work in groups.** In the video, you saw a historical mash-up, the Great Sphinx of Giza. Use the Internet to learn more about the Great Sphinx. Present the information to the class.

103

Count and noncount nouns: Talking about amounts

Count nouns

A few / Some / A lot of / Many meal**s are** a mix of food from different cultures.

How many chef**s combine** foods from different cultures?

Two / A few / Some / A lot of / Many chefs **combine** foods from different cultures.

Restaurants usually have **a couple of / three / too many** special dish**es**.

Noncount nouns

A little / Some / A lot of / Much fruit **is** used in food from different cultures.

How much cheese **is** on a Japanese-Italian pizza?

A little / Some / A lot of cheese.

Dessert sushi sometimes has **a piece of / some / too much** fruit in it.

30 **Work in pairs.** Choose the correct word or phrase to complete the sentences.

Maiza: We had _____ (a few / some) delicious KoMex food last night.

Gabi: KoMex? In other words, Korean and Mexican food combined, right? Did they have Korean tacos?

Maiza: Yes, and _____ (much / a few) different kinds. I like beef tacos. Their tacos had

_____ (a lot of / a few) Korean barbecue

beef and _____ (a couple of / much) cucumber slices on fresh corn tortillas. Oh,

and _____ (some / many) great sauce, too.

KoMex food

Gabi: Mmm. Sounds good. How _____ (much / many) tacos did you eat?

Maiza: Not too _____ (many / much). I only had _____ (one / a little)

taco, but I had _____ (much / a lot of) nachos. They had Korean meat and mango salsa.

Gabi: Sounds great! And did you try _____ (a couple of / some) kimchi rice?

Maiza: I only ate _____ (a few / a little). I was full!

31 **Work in groups.** Toss the cubes. Ask and answer questions about how people in the country eat or drink the item on the cube.

How much rice do you think people in Japan eat?

I think they eat a lot of rice.

Go to p. 167.

When you write a paragraph of exemplification, you introduce an idea. Then you use examples to support that idea. The following phrases can help you introduce examples:

for example   **one/another example is**   **such as**

32 **Read the model.** Work in pairs to find and underline phrases that introduce examples.

Ani-mixes

Combining photos of two or more animals is a popular activity these days. There are a lot of funny and weird animal mixes that people create and share on the Internet. For example, a "turger" is a tiger with a turtle shell. Another example is the "dish," which is a mix of a dog and a fish. Its body has a few fins and some scales, and it has a lot of fur on its dog head. Some mixes are a little scary, such as the "sharilla." It's a combination of a shark and a gorilla, with the head of a shark and the body of a gorilla. It has a huge mouth with a lot of teeth in it. It has a huge, furry body, and its head and fur are almost the same color. It's funny to look at, but I think I'd run if I saw a "sharilla" in real life!

A "sharilla"

33 **Discuss in pairs.** What are the three animal mixes you read about? How would you react to seeing each of them?

34 **Write.** Create your own unique ani-mix. Name it and write a paragraph about it. Give examples of what makes it unique. If possible, create a photo and include it with your paragraph.

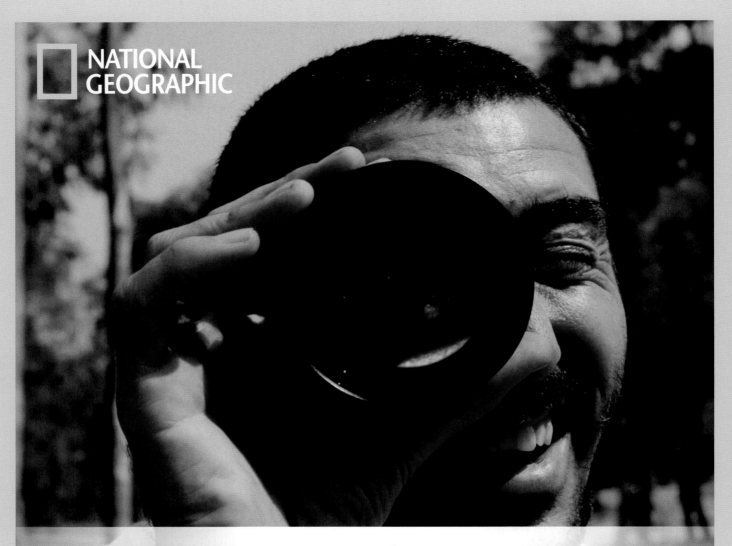

Be Unique

"Look where everyone is looking, then turn 180 degrees and walk. You'll often find that's where the gems are."

—Josh Ponte

National Geographic Explorer, Musical Explorer/Filmmaker

1. **Watch scene 6.2.**

2. When people learned that Josh planned to quit his job and work in Gabon, many of them thought he was taking a big risk. Do you agree? Why or why not?

3. Think of a time when you did something really different from what everyone else was doing. What did you do? Was it easy or difficult? Were you glad you did it? Why or why not?

Make an Impact

A **Make and explain food art.**

· Decide what to create and what food to use.

· Photograph each step as you create your art.

· Share your photographs with the class. Explain how you made your artwork.

B **Create a mash-up comic strip.**

· Choose any two types of stories to mix for your mash-up. For example, mix a fairy tale and science fiction.

· Write the story in six to eight panels. Draw pictures in each panel.

· Share your story with the class.

C **Invent a hybrid sport.**

· Choose two or three sports you like. Think of how to combine them.

· Write rules for your sport.

· Explain your sport. If possible, demonstrate it for the class.

Express Yourself

1 Read and listen to learn how to create a steampunk outfit. TR: 87

Steampunk

Steampunk combines the fashion of Victorian England (1837–1901) with science fiction. The *steam* in steampunk refers to steam-powered machinery from the nineteenth century. *Punk* means breaking traditional rules.

2 Discuss in groups.

1. Do you like the steampunk look? What do you think is interesting about it? What don't you like? Explain.

2. Where do you get ideas about fashion?

Get steampunked. Here's how:

Plan Think about the character you want. Do you want to be a pilot? Or maybe a sailor? How about a scientist or a soldier? Choosing a character will help you select the best clothing and accessories.

Create Now think about what you'll wear: old-fashioned pants and a jacket, or maybe a beautiful dress. Be creative! Make changes you want to create something unique. For example, Victorian-era women wore high-heeled boots, but you might prefer flat shoes. Your clothes can be in any color, though many fans of steampunk prefer dark colors.

Steampunk it! Now for the important part—accessories! If you have an outfit that looks Victorian but doesn't have accessories, it's not steampunk! Steampunk accessories can include goggles, machine parts, old watches, leather belts, or interesting hats. Remember to choose accessories that match your character.

3) **Connect ideas.** In Unit 5, you learned about fashion. In Unit 6, you learned about combining things to make something new. What connection do you see between the two units?

4) **Choose an activity.**

1. Choose a topic:
   - fashion
   - mash-ups

2. Choose a way to express yourself:
   - a magazine article
   - a fashion show
   - a video

3. Present your work.

Cool Apps and Gadgets

A rider using special LED
lights on his bicycle wheels
for safety, Hong Kong

The biggest thing we're trying to
do is to make people curious."
—Manu Prakash

1. Look at the photograph. Why do you think the rider
   added lights to his bicycle?

2. What electronics are important to you? Which ones
   do you use every day? Which would you like that you
   don't have now?

3. How do you think the electronics you use now will
   change in the future?

More and more people have begun to use electronic gadgets. Why do you think this is?

Discuss. Then listen and read. TR: 88

It's incredible to think that people haven't even been using the **Internet** for 30 years. When the Internet was first used, you had to **connect** through a telephone line and it could be very slow. Things have changed a lot since then. Today nearly four billion people have a **mobile gadget**, such as a **smartphone**, a tablet, or both. And with **Wi-Fi** in many public spaces, it's easier than ever to connect.

Many agree that mobile gadgets and the **apps** on them are **useful**. They make our lives so much easier. We can do things like **search** for a word in the dictionary or use a flashlight with just the swipe of a finger! At any time and place, we can **send** and receive e-mails, play **games**, or **look up** information. We can also **share** photos and videos or **chat** with friends and family using mobile technology. Smartphones have made it possible to send texts. By 2015, people were sending eight trillion texts per year. It's now the most popular way to communicate.

Because it's so useful, people spend a lot of time on the Internet. Probably too much time! In fact, the average person is online for almost four and a half hours each day. We connect to the Internet with a smartphone more than any other device. Some people worry that we spend too much time with our gadgets. What about you? Do you spend too much time on the Internet?

Areas marked in red show the highest rate of Internet use. Areas marked in blue show a low rate of Internet use.

2 **Learn new words.** Listen and repeat. TR: 89

3 **Work in pairs.** How much time do you spend on the Internet every day? How does this compare with the average Internet user?

113

Thinking Outside the BOX

Young inventor Brooke Martin on the screen of an iCPooch

17 **Before you read, discuss in pairs.** Look at the photo. Describe what you think the gadget does.

18 **Learn new words.** Find these words in the reading. What do you think they mean? Think about what type of word each one is. Then listen and repeat. TR: 98

to borrow	to find
function	to invent

19 **While you read, look for the main idea and details that support it.** TR: 99

20 **After you read, work in pairs.** Check *T* for true statements or *F* for false statements.

1. All you need for Bot2Karot is a smartphone app. **T** **F**

2. Bot2Karot helps people take care of their gardens. **T** **F**

3. Brooke Martin was sixteen when she invented iCPooch. **T** **F**

4. The only thing you can do with iCPooch is look at your dog. **T** **F**

5. Robert Saunt likes playing video games. **T** **F**

6. Robert's gadget will be good for the environment. **T** **F**

118

If you think young people can't have an impact on the world, think again. Over the years, teens have invented remarkable things that solve problems and have changed the ways people do things. And they're going to continue to invent things in the future.

Take fourteen-year-old Eliott Sarrey from France, for example. He invented Bot2Karot, a gardening robot that can take care of a small vegetable garden. The robot is controlled by an app on a smartphone. It helps people grow and take care of vegetables. It also saves water and energy, and makes gardening easy for people who are very busy or have difficulty getting around.

Brooke Martin is an animal lover who missed her dog when she was away. She also knew that her dog suffered from stress when its owners left. So Brooke invented iCPooch® when she was just twelve years old. The iCPooch lets pet owners check on their pets from anywhere in the world using a tablet or a smartphone. This award-winning gadget also allows owners to use their smartphone camera to video chat with their pets. It has another function, too. Owners can quickly and easily give their pet a treat by touching the *drop cookie* button on their screen. Dogs and owners must be pretty grateful to Brooke for this invention!

Fourteen-year-old inventor Robert Saunt was tired of buying or borrowing different video-game controllers for each game console. So he invented a controller called *Game Blox*. It can be used with four of the most popular game consoles. His invention will save players a lot of money and space, and it will save 330 million kg (727 million lb.) of materials every year. Players will also be able to listen to music while they play video games with Robert's gadget.

Kids all over the world find ways to solve problems every day. Who knows? Maybe the next time you have a problem, you'll come up with the next amazing idea!

21 **Discuss your answers to Activity 19 in small groups.** Then complete the following:

Main idea

_____

_____

Detail 1

_____

_____

Detail 2

_____

_____

Detail 3

_____

_____

22 **Discuss in groups.**

1. Which of these three inventions do you think is the most useful? Why? Which do you think is the least useful? Why?

2. What do you think is the greatest invention of all time? Who invented it? Why is it so great?

3. Brooke worried about her dog when she was on vacation. Think of two other ways she could check on her dog while she's away.

23 **Before you watch, discuss in pairs.** Before smartphones and other new electronic gadgets, how did people tell time? Take photos? Listen to music?

24 **Read and circle.** You're going to watch *From Gadgets to Apps*. From the title, predict the main idea of the video. Circle the letter.

a. Gadgets are more important than their apps.
b. Useful apps are replacing gadgets.
c. We will use different gadgets and apps in the future.

25 Watch scene 7.1. **While you watch, complete the chart.**

Function	Today	What people first used for this function	The problem with the original gadget
tell time	clock app		
listen to music	music app		
take a photo	camera app		

26 **After you watch, match the two parts of the sentences.**

_____ 1. The digital age

_____ 2. Watches in the 1950s

_____ 3. Before there were instant cameras, people

_____ 4. Instant cameras

_____ 5. In the 1950s, gadgets for listening to music

a. were easy to use but only made one copy of a photo.

b. were small and portable but had only one use.

c. were smaller than before, but they still couldn't fit in our pockets.

d. actually began in the 1950s.

e. depended on professional photographers.

120

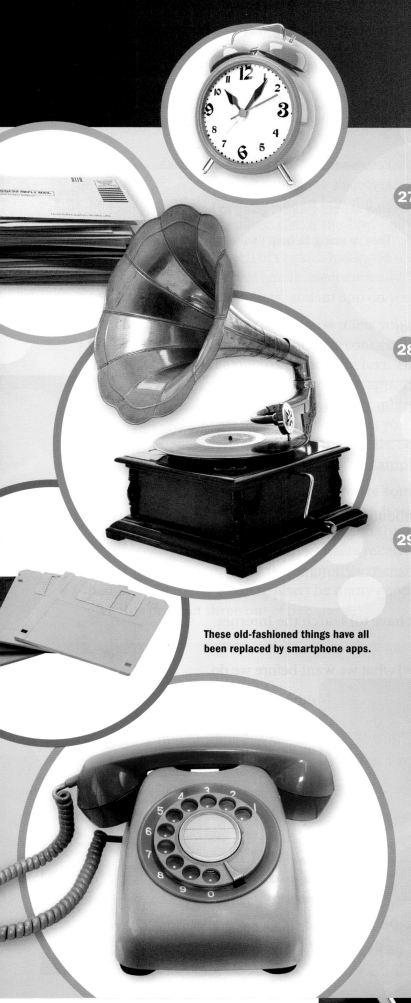

These old-fashioned things have all been replaced by smartphone apps.

27 **Work in pairs.** In the video, you heard, "Your phone might have an app for giving you directions to a friend's house, but you can't ride it there." Think of three apps you like. What things can they do? What can't they do? Discuss.

28 **Discuss in groups.**

1. At the end of the video, you're asked, "What other gadgets do you use? Why are they useful? Will there ever be apps for them?" Answer these questions.

2. What old-fashioned item or gadget is still used in your home? Why is it useful?

29 **Choose an activity.**

1. **Work independently.** Find out about the lives of people in your country one hundred years ago. How did they communicate? Travel from place to place? Take photos? Get information? Share what you learn with the class.

2. **Work in pairs.** Role-play a historical figure and a teenager of today. The teen must show and explain how a certain gadget works. The historical figure must react and ask questions appropriate for his/her time period.

3. **Work in groups.** Choose an activity that you do on your smartphone, such as listening to music or taking photos. Use the Internet to find out about how this activity was done at different times in the past. Make a timeline to show how the activity has changed.

121

Always Keep Learning

"It's valuable to know what you don't know, and there's so much we don't know."

—Manu Prakash

National Geographic Explorer, Biophysicist

1. Watch scene 7.2.

2. Manu made a microscope that was cheap and easy to carry. How could this microscope be useful to a student like you? What could you learn if you had access to a microscope wherever you were?

3. Name something that you're interested in, but don't know a lot about. What would you like to learn about it? How could you learn this information?

Make an Impact

A Plan and give a presentation about the future.

· Take photos of five things in your house that you think we won't
  use or that will be very different ten years from now.
· Prepare a presentation about what will replace these things or
  how they'll change and why.
· Present your ideas to the class.

B Design a robot.

· Think about a task you don't like doing. Design a robot to do that task.
· Draw and label a picture of your robot.
· Present your robot to the class. Explain how it will work.

C Create an "outdated gadget museum."

· Collect five or six items that were useful in
  the past but have been replaced by smartphones.
· Arrange the items in a "museum."
  Write descriptions of the items,
  including when they were invented
  and when they became less popular.
· Display your museum in class.
  Answer your classmates'
  questions about each item.

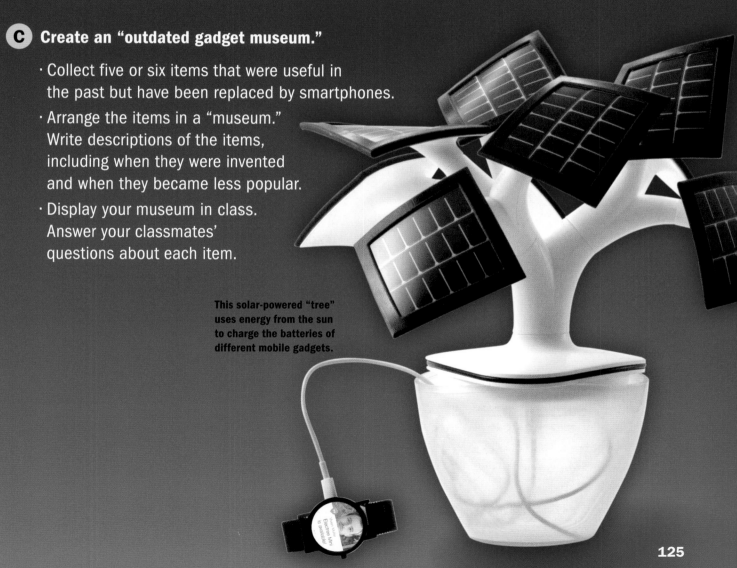

This solar-powered "tree"
uses energy from the sun
to charge the batteries of
different mobile gadgets.

Into the Past

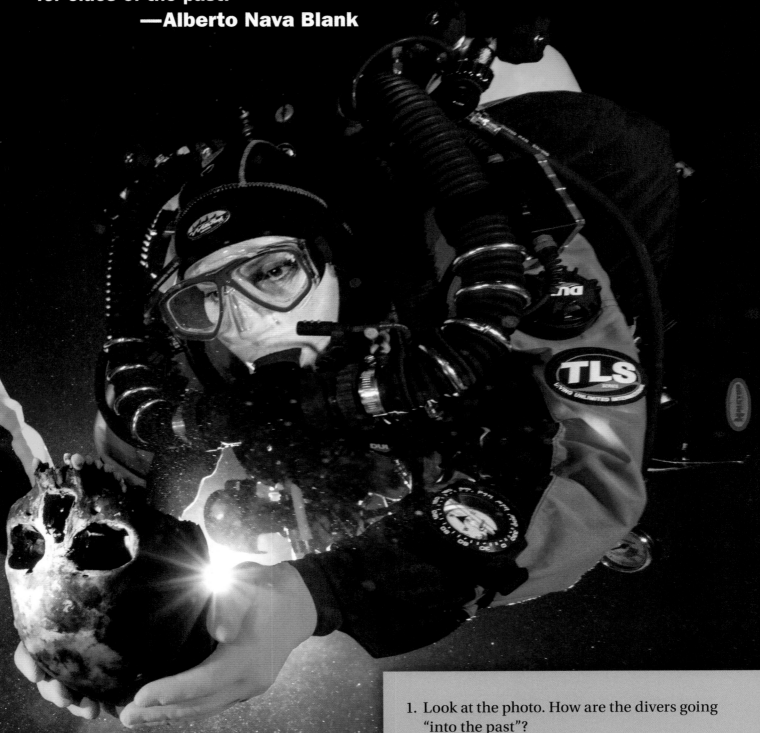

"It's human nature to explore and learn about ourselves by searching for clues of the past."
—**Alberto Nava Blank**

In the Hoyo Negro cenote in Mexico, divers Alberto Nava Blank and Susan Bird find the skull of Naia, a teenage girl who lived approximately 13,000 years ago.

1. Look at the photo. How are the divers going "into the past"?

2. Why do you think researchers try to understand the past?

3. Are you interested in learning about people who lived before you? Why or why not?

17 **Before you read, discuss in pairs.** Look at the girl in the photo. How do you think her life was different from yours?

18 **Learn new words.** Find these words in the reading. What do you think they mean? Look for their definitions or examples in the text. Then listen and repeat. TR: 112

| age | chore | culture | education | teenager |

19 **While you read, think about cause and effect.** TR: 113

20 **After you read, work in pairs to answer the questions.**

1. What culture thought that education was very important?
2. Why couldn't some parents teach their children at home?
3. At what age did people start getting married?
4. How often did children work in factories?
5. At what age did children begin working in factories?
6. What did children do with the money they made?

21 **Complete the chart.**

Cause	Effect
	Most children didn't go to school from 500–1500.
Aztecs believed that education was important.	
	Children began working in factories in cities.

22 **Work in groups.**

1. What would be the hardest thing for you if you were growing up in the past? Why?
2. Interview an older person about his or her life as a teenager. How was it the same as your life now? How was it different?
3. Why do you think the lives of children around the world have improved from long ago? Give three reasons. Do you think it's worse in any way today? Explain.

Growing Up:
THEN AND NOW

How kids' lives have changed over the years

What's a day in your life like today? You go to school and do your homework, right? At home, you probably do a few simple chores, like washing the dishes or making your bed. You might complain about not having enough free time to relax.

In the past, kids your age probably had a little more to complain about. Throughout much of history, many didn't go to school because they had to help all day at home or on the farm. Their parents taught them what they knew, but very few adults could read or write. The Aztec people, who lived from 1200 to 1473 in present-day Mexico, were unique. The Aztecs believed that education, or learning, was important. Every child went to school, although boys and girls learned different things.

People married and had children when they were young in Aztec culture. This was true in Europe, as well. There, girls often married as young as twelve and boys as young as fourteen. In both cultures, these teenagers rarely chose who they married.

By the nineteenth century, many people began moving into cities to find jobs. In cities, there was no longer a need to have children work on the farm. So instead, they began working in factories. In England, many children worked long hours six days a week. And they earned as little as a penny a day— that's less than fifty cents in today's money! Children started working from a very young age, sometimes at only five or six years old. They gave all of their money to their parents to help pay for the family's needs.

Today most children go to school. Sometimes teenagers work part-time jobs to earn money. But many use that money for enjoyment, not to help their families. Think about it! Even if you work and go to school, you still have time to relax or hang out with your friends. Next to your peers from the past, you have it pretty easy!

A girl working in a factory, 1908

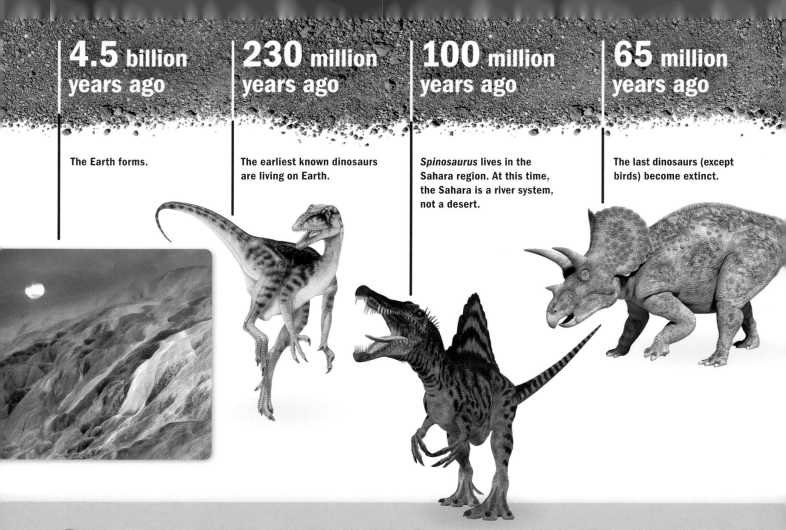

4.5 billion years ago

The Earth forms.

230 million years ago

The earliest known dinosaurs are living on Earth.

100 million years ago

Spinosaurus lives in the Sahara region. At this time, the Sahara is a river system, not a desert.

65 million years ago

The last dinosaurs (except birds) become extinct.

23 **Before you watch, discuss in pairs.** Earlier in the unit, you learned about our human ancestors. But Earth has existed for much longer than humans and our ancestors. What do you know about life on Earth before humans?

24 **Work in pairs.** You are going to watch *A Journey Back in Time*. The explorer, Nizar Ibrahim, makes a discovery about life before humans. Look at the photo of Nizar (the last photo on the timeline). What do you think he discovered?

25 Watch scene 8.1. **While you watch, check your predictions from Activity 24.**

26 **After you watch, work in pairs to answer the questions.**

1. Today the Sahara Desert is full of sand. What was it like 100 million years ago?
2. What was Nizar looking for?
3. Where did he work? Why did people think he was foolish to work there?
4. He found part of a skeleton. What type of creature did it belong to?
5. During the time of dinosaurs, what important group was **not** on Earth?

4.4 million years ago

Early human ancestors (*Ardipithecus ramidus*) are living in present-day Ethiopia.

2.5 million years ago

Our human ancestors begin using stone tools, a sign of advanced intelligence.

100,000 years ago

Our ancestors have evolved into our current species, *Homo sapiens*.

Present-day

Modern humans have the tools and technology to study and understand the past.

27 **Discuss in pairs.**

1. Look at the timeline. How many years separate the last dinosaurs from the earliest humans? What do you think happened during this period?

2. Nizar says that holding dinosaur fossils is like holding "a snapshot in time." What would be exciting about holding something so old?

28 **Choose an activity.**

1. **Work independently.** Nizar describes the Sahara as "a magical place, both beautiful and frightening, peaceful and cruel." Think of another place that is beautiful and peaceful, but can still be frightening. Describe this place to the class. If possible, share a photo.

2. **Work in pairs.** In the video, Nizar imagines the world when dinosaurs lived. Discuss how you imagine the world at this time. Draw a picture and share it with the class.

3. **Work in groups.** Create a short story or comic book about life during the time of the dinosaurs. Share your work with the class.

137

There + to be: Expressing existence at different points of time

There have always **been** sun celebrations around the world.

However, **there wasn't** a Festival of the Sun in Peru after the Spanish arrived.

Now **there's** a Festival of the Sun every year.

Are there going to be traditional musicians?

Will there be a lot of people?

There has been a Festival of the Sun in Peru for centuries.

There weren't any other traditional Incan festivals at that time, either.

There are a lot of different foods to try.

Yes, **there are going to be** dancers, too.

I think **there will be**. It's very popular.

29 **Read and complete the dialogue.** Use *there* + the correct form of *to be*.

Juan: Andrea, you're from Peru, right?
          _____ a lot of
          fun things to do during your country's
          Festival of the Sun?

Andrea: Yes, _____ . The
          festival is called *Inti Raymi*. It's a week
          long, and _____
          live concerts and shows. In fact,
          _____ only one festival in South America that's bigger!

An Inti Raymi celebration

Juan: Really? It sounds amazing!

Andrea: Oh, it is. Last year _____ about 150,000 people in the town
          of Cuzco watching the ceremony. _____ 500 actors in the
          ceremony. They really brought the past to life.

Juan: Cool! Does the history of this festival go back a long time?

Andrea: Oh, yes! _____ Inti Raymi celebrations since the 1500s.

Juan: _____ a festival next year?

Andrea: Yes, _____ . It's held every year.

30 **Work in pairs.** Think of a festival you have been to. Describe the festival with as many details as possible. Use *there* with the correct form of *to be*.

31 **Work in groups.** Choose a celebration you all know about. Turn over a card. Try to be the first to slap the card and make a sentence about that celebration.

There will be . . .

Go to p. 175.

138

WRITING

When you write a classification paragraph, you divide your main topic into different parts. You give details and examples about each of the parts. When you finish, write a concluding sentence to connect the parts to the main topic.

32 **Read the model.** What is the main topic? How many parts does the writer divide the paragraph into?

> The summer solstice, the first day of summer, has always been a special day. There have been summer solstice celebrations since ancient times. Some of these are still celebrated today. In Sweden, people celebrate this, the longest day of the year, by singing, dancing around a maypole, and enjoying special food and drinks. Unlike Sweden, people in Spain don't dance around a maypole. Instead, they dance in the streets. There are fireworks and bonfires. Some people even jump over the bonfires. People in both Sweden and Spain celebrate the summer solstice at the end of the day. However, at Stonehenge in the United Kingdom, thousands of people come together to celebrate at sunrise. They wear masks and costumes. The sounds of beating drums fill the air at this celebration. People around the world celebrate the summer solstice in different ways that reflect their culture.

33 **Work in pairs.** What are the different parts of the paragraph? What does the writer describe in each part?

34 **Write.** Write a paragraph about a traditional festival or celebration from your culture. Write three details or examples and a concluding sentence.

A summer solstice celebration
at Stonehenge, United Kingdom

Understand the Past

"The underwater caves of the Yucatán Peninsula are a time capsule of what human lives were like 10,000 years ago."

—Alberto Nava Blank
National Geographic Explorer, Underwater Cave Explorer/Cartographer

1. **Watch scene 8.2.**

2. A time capsule is a collection of artifacts that represent a certain period of time. What are three things that you might find in a time capsule from 10,000 years ago? 1,000 years ago? 10 years ago?

3. Think of life in your country 100 years ago. What was harder back then? What was better?

Make an Impact

A **Teach the class to play mancala.**

· Research the history of mancala. Learn how to play. Write the instructions on a poster.

· Make mancala boards for your classmates. Use egg cartons. Bring in seeds or beans as pieces.

· Share your poster and teach classmates how to play mancala. Walk around to answer any questions as others play the game.

B **Make a biographical poster.**

· Research a scientist who discovered something connected to our human origins.

· Prepare a biography of that person. Include information on what he or she discovered, and what it taught us about our human origins.

· Create a poster and share the information with the class.

C **Perform a skit.**

· Choose a time period in the past, and research what kids did then.

· Write and rehearse a skit showing what life was like for kids at that time. Find costumes and props.

· Perform the skit for your classmates.

Mancala

Express Yourself

Read and listen to a student's predictions for the future. TR: 115

Dear "future friend,"

I'm writing this letter for my school's time capsule. I want to include my predictions for the future, instead of describing the present. I love to think about the future, especially how people will get around.

I bet that there will be some cool ways to travel in the future. For example, people will be able to live in one city and work in another because we'll be able to travel in small pods that move really fast —more than 1,200 kph (750 mph)— through a special tunnel. Just like in airplanes, there will be screens on the backs of seats so passengers can relax and watch movies as they travel. And the best thing will be that the vehicles that travel in this tunnel will use energy from the sun, so they'll be better for the environment.

Transportation will do more than just move us around quickly. It will take us out of this world! People are already talking about traveling to Mars. I bet that in the future it will take about four to six months to get there. Then travelers will stay about two years. Of course, going to Mars won't be for everyone. If people just want to look at Earth from above, they'll be able to take an elevator into space!

When you read this letter, please check how many of my predictions have come true. Who knows? Maybe I'll be able to time travel to find out myself!

Maria

A space elevator

2. **Discuss in groups.**

1. Have you ever seen a time capsule? If so, what was in it? If not, would you be interested in one? Why or why not?

2. What would you put in a time capsule to be opened in 100 years?

3. Which forms of transportation that Maria mentions would you like to take? Why?

3. **Connect ideas.** In Unit 7, you learned about life with modern gadgets. In Unit 8, you learned about people, tools, and games from long ago. What connection do you see between the two units?

4. **Choose an activity.**

1. Choose a topic:
   - tools and games of today and tomorrow
   - tools and games of the past

2. Choose a way to express yourself:
   - a letter for a time capsule
   - a video presentation
   - a skit

3. Present your work.

Unit 1

Syllables and stress

1 **Listen.** Words in English have one or more parts. These parts make up *syllables*. A syllable has a vowel sound and can also have one or more consonant sounds. Listen. Notice the numbers of syllables in these words. **TR: 116**

1	2	3
☐	☐ ☐	☐ ☐ ☐
man	Ja - **pan**	Ja - pa - **nese**
street	**peo**-ple	**ci** - ti - zen
bridge	**brid**-ges	**na**-tion-al

In words with two or more syllables, one syllable is stronger than the others. The vowel in that syllable is pronounced more loudly and clearly. This is the stressed syllable. Listen again and notice the stressed syllable in the two- and three-syllable words above.

2 **Listen and repeat.** Do the word pairs have the same number of syllables? Write *Y* for *yes* or *N* for *no*. Then listen again and circle the stressed syllable. **TR: 117**

1. __Y__ (Lon)don — (Eng)land
2. _____ surround — surrounded
3. _____ Mexico — America
4. _____ travel — traveled
5. _____ sidewalk — highway
6. _____ explore — exploration

3 **Work in pairs.** Write the words in the correct column. Then listen to the completed chart to check your answers. **TR: 118**

~~architecture~~	design	planned	sign
entertainment	capital	resident	unique

1 syllable	2 syllables	3 syllables	4 syllables
			architecture

Unit 2

Intonation in questions

1 **Listen.** Notice how the voice goes up or down at the end of the questions. **TR: 119**

Does a pastry chef wear a uniform? ↗

Do pastry chefs work every day? ↗

How do you create beautiful desserts? ↘

Where do pastry chefs work? ↘

The voice rises at the end of questions asking for an answer of *yes* or *no*.

The voice falls at the end of questions that ask for information. These questions start with the words *who, what, when, where, why,* and *how.*

2 **Listen and repeat.** Circle the correct arrow to indicate intonation for each question. **TR: 120**

1. Where does he work? ↗ (↘)
2. Does she work full time? ↗ ↘
3. Who is your boss? ↗ ↘
4. Is this design yours? ↗ ↘
5. Do they like their jobs? ↗ ↘
6. When do you finish work? ↗ ↘

3 **Work in pairs.** Does the voice go up or down at the end of these questions? Draw an arrow. Then ask and answer the questions.

(Do you like cake?) (Yes, of course I do!)

1. Do you like cake? ↗
2. When do you have English class?
3. Do you have a busy schedule?
4. Do you do your homework every day?
5. What do you do on the weekends?

Unit 3

Present progressive: Stress of the verb *be*

1 **Listen.** Notice the pronunciation of the forms of *be*. TR: 121

Akiko **isn't** sleeping.
Some animals <u>are</u> hunting.

<u>Are</u> they going to the festival?
Yes, they **are**.

<u>Is</u> she eating breakfast now?
Yes, she **is**. And we'<u>re</u> going to bed!

Be is unstressed when it's in an affirmative statement or a question.

Be is stressed when it's in a negative statement or at the end of a short answer.

2 **Listen and repeat.** Circle the stressed forms of *be*. TR: 122

1. A: When is the sun coming out?
   B: It isn't coming out!
2. A: Is it raining?
   B: Yes, it is.
3. A: Which animals are sleeping now?
   B: Bears and bats.
4. A: Are the children skiing?
   B: No, they aren't.

3 **Work in pairs.** Listen and repeat the questions. Then ask and answer them with a partner. Be sure to stress *be* when necessary. TR: 123

> What are you studying this week?

> We're studying Norway.

1. What are you studying this week?
2. Are you enjoying this weather?
3. Who are you studying with now?
4. When are you taking your next test?
5. Is your teacher smiling?

Unit 4

Can and *can't*

1 **Listen.** Notice the pronunciation of *can* and *can't*. TR: 124

<u>Can</u> an alligator run?
Yes, it **can**. But you <u>can</u> run faster.

How <u>can</u> people help sea turtles?
They <u>can</u> help protect their nests.

I **can't** believe Amy's story about the lion! <u>Can</u> you?
No, I **can't**! It's amazing.

In statements and questions, *can* sounds like *kn*. The vowel *a* is weak.

In short answers and negative contractions, the vowel *a* is strong. It's pronounced fully. For example:

I **can't** see. Can you?
Yes, I **can**.

2 **Listen and repeat.** Cross out the *a* in the weak forms of *can*. TR: 125

1. People <u>can</u> help animals in many ways.
2. <u>Can</u> the city build an animal crossing this year?
   No, they <u>can't</u>. They don't have the money.
3. Elephants <u>can</u> walk under the road in Kenya.
4. Many animals <u>can't</u> safely cross roads.
5. The red crabs <u>can</u> cross the road safely now, so they <u>can't</u> be harmed anymore.

3 **Work in pairs.** Listen and repeat the questions. Then ask and answer them. TR: 126

> Can you milk a cow or goat?

> No, I can't! Can you?

1. Can you milk a cow or goat?
2. Can you keep a baboon as a pet?
3. Where can I get a kitten?
4. What animals can we help in this country?
5. Can you make animal noises in English?

Unit 5

The -ed ending

1 **Listen.** Notice the different pronunciations for each -ed ending. TR: 127

ed	t	d
wanted	looked	learned
needed	dressed	changed
protected	helped	loved

The -ed ending has three possible pronunciations:

- ed sound when the final sound of a verb is t or d
- t sound when the final sound of a verb is f, k, p, s, sh, ch, and x
- d sound when the final sound of a verb is a vowel or any other consonant

2 **Listen and repeat the words.** Then write the number of syllables in each word. TR: 128

1. _1_ played   4. ___ created   7. ___ needed
2. ___ climbed   5. ___ picked   8. ___ asked
3. ___ waited   6. ___ reached   9. ___ protected

3 **Listen and repeat.** Then write each word in the correct column. Listen to check your answers. TR: 129 and 130

added	attached	believed	colored
decided	dried	graduated	mixed
produced	saved	washed	wasted

ed	t	d
added		

Unit 6

Linking: Consonant + vowel sounds

1 **Listen.** Notice how the words join together. TR: 131

Who is it?

I give up.

What has the body of a lion?

When a word ending in a consonant sound comes before a word beginning with a vowel sound, the final consonant sound often links to the vowel. It sounds like one long word.

2 **Listen and repeat.** Draw a link from the final consonant sound to the vowel. TR: 132

1. It's amazing!   4. was it   7. planned anything
2. made up   5. think I   8. What's up?
3. have a   6. love it

3 **Work in pairs.** Complete the conversation with phrases from Activity 2. Listen to check your answers. TR: 133

Jane: Hi, Kim! ___What's up?___

Kim: I just _____ a history test.

Jane: How _____ ?

Kim: Difficult! I _____ passed, though.

Jane: That's good. So have you _____ for your birthday yet?

Kim: Not yet. I want to _____ party at the new Korean restaurant. Do you like karaoke?

Jane: I _____ ! What's Korean food like?

Kim: _____

Unit 7

The two-vowel rule

1 **Listen.** Notice how the vowels in these words are pronounced like the first vowel. TR: 134

a	e	i	o	u
p<u>ai</u>d	r<u>ea</u>d	d<u>i</u>e	r<u>oa</u>d	d<u>ue</u>
b<u>a</u>ke	P<u>e</u>te	b<u>i</u>ke	b<u>o</u>ne	t<u>u</u>ne

As a rule, when two vowels are in the same word or syllable, the second vowel is silent. The letter name is the sound. For example, in the words *paid* and *bake*, the sound is like the name of the letter *A*.

Although there are exceptions, this is true most of the time.

2 **Listen and repeat.** Circle the word where the two-vowel rule does not work. TR: 135

1. seat, beach, (great), peach, team
2. save, have, wave, shave, behave
3. some, phone, home, joke, bone
4. oat, soap, road, boat, roar
5. cute, cube, Tuesday, statue, duet
6. train, said, paid, rain, explain

3 **Work in pairs.** Look at pp. 112–113. Find words that follow the two-vowel rule. Write as many of them as you can in two minutes.

a	e	i	o	u

Unit 8

The schwa (/ə/) sound

1 **Listen.** Notice the pronunciation of the underlined vowels. TR: 136

Chin<u>a</u>   stud<u>e</u>nt   fam<u>i</u>ly

t<u>o</u>night   helpf<u>u</u>l   act<u>io</u>n

As you've learned, when a word in English has two or more syllables, one is stronger, or stressed. The vowel in a stressed syllable is clearly pronounced.

Vowel sounds in unstressed syllables are not fully pronounced and often do not sound like the letter in the word. Many unstressed syllables have the *schwa* sound.

Schwa is a relaxed *uh* sound. The symbol in dictionaries looks like an upside-down *e* (/ə/). Schwa is the most common sound in the English language.

2 **Listen.** Complete the schwa sounds in these words with the missing vowels. Then listen again and repeat. TR: 137 and 138

1. She's an ____dult. They are her childr____n.
2. I made my fam____ly tree because I want to know where I came from.
3. The Ice Man lived in anc____ ____nt times.
4. These days, life is not as diffic____lt for kids as it was in the past, but some still c____mplain!
5. J____pan is in As____ ____ .
6. The U.S. is in North ____meric____ .

3 **Work in pairs.** Listen and repeat these words. Circle the syllables with the schwa sound. Compare your answers. Then take turns saying the words. TR: 139

(a)go   de scen dant   o ri gin

sym bol   fe sti val   pro ba bly

con trol   na tion   ske le ton

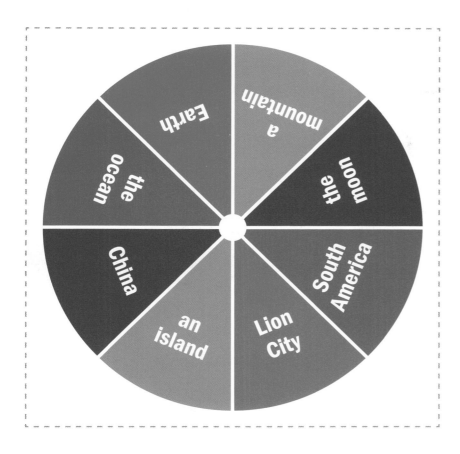

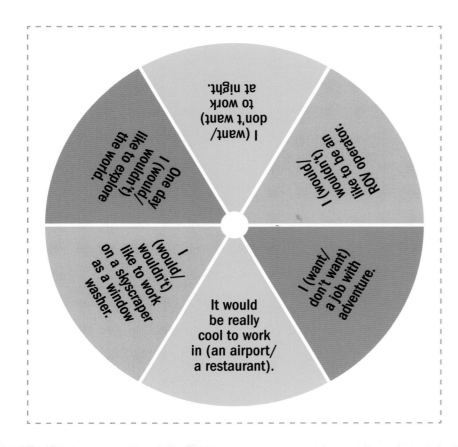

It's a **kakapo**.
Pronounced: *kah-kuh-poh*

It lives for about 60 years.

It's an **herbivore**.
- Pronounced: *ur-buh-vohr*
- Eats only plants

Tell me about
this animal.

It's a **zorilla**.
Pronounced: *zuh-rii-uh*

It lives in Africa.

It's a **carnivore**.
- Pronounced: *kar-nuh-vor*
- Eats mostly meat

Tell me about
this animal.

It's a **bandicoot**.
Pronounced: *ban-di-koot*

It eats both plants and animals.

It's a **marsupial**.
- Pronounced: *mar-soo-pee-uhl*
- Carries its babies in a pocket or pouch

Tell me about
this animal.

It's a **vinegaroon**.
Pronounced: *vin-i-guh-roon*

It has strong claws for catching food.

It's an **arachnid**.
- Pronounced: *uh-rak-nid*
- Like a spider

Tell me about
this animal.

It's a **Gila monster**.
Pronounced: *hee-la mon-ster*

It's nocturnal in the hot summers.

It's **venomous**.
- Pronounced: *ven-uh-muss*
- Poisonous

Tell me about
this animal.

It's a **tarsier**.
Pronounced: *tahr-see-ey*

It spends most of its time in trees.

It's an unusual **mammal**.
- Pronounced: *mam-uhl*
- Feeds its babies with milk

Tell me about
this animal.

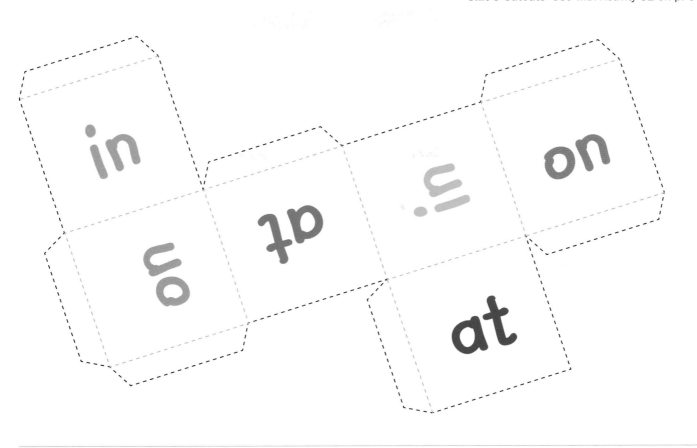

can	couldn't	could
could	WILD	can't
couldn't	can	can't

Elephants don't like to walk through chili pepper bushes.

Amy Dickman started the Ruaha Carnivore Project.

Tigers attack people on the tiger reserves in India.

Amy Dickman is helping the villagers protect their animals.

Big cats in Tanzania hunt the village farmers' animals.

Baboons in Cape Town go into people's kitchens.

Humans and wild animals are interacting more often.

There are baboon monitors in Cape Town.

Humans need protection from wildlife.

People hunt leopards in Central Asia.

Start

End

Our clothes **show/don't show** who we really are.

We **should/ shouldn't** be allowed to wear jeans to school.

You shared a lot of opinions. Congratulations!

Casual clothes **should/ shouldn't** replace formal clothes in all situations.

You didn't wear your school uniform today. Lose a turn!

Fashion **will/ won't** change much in the next century.

Boys **should/ shouldn't** wear ties to school.

Dressing up **is/ isn't** fun.

Fashion is **more/less** important than being practical.

Students of different ages **should/shouldn't** wear the same uniforms.

You look great in your formal clothes! Move ahead one space.

Jeans and a sweatshirt **are/aren't** the best clothes for school.

Your clothes aren't very practical. Go back to start!

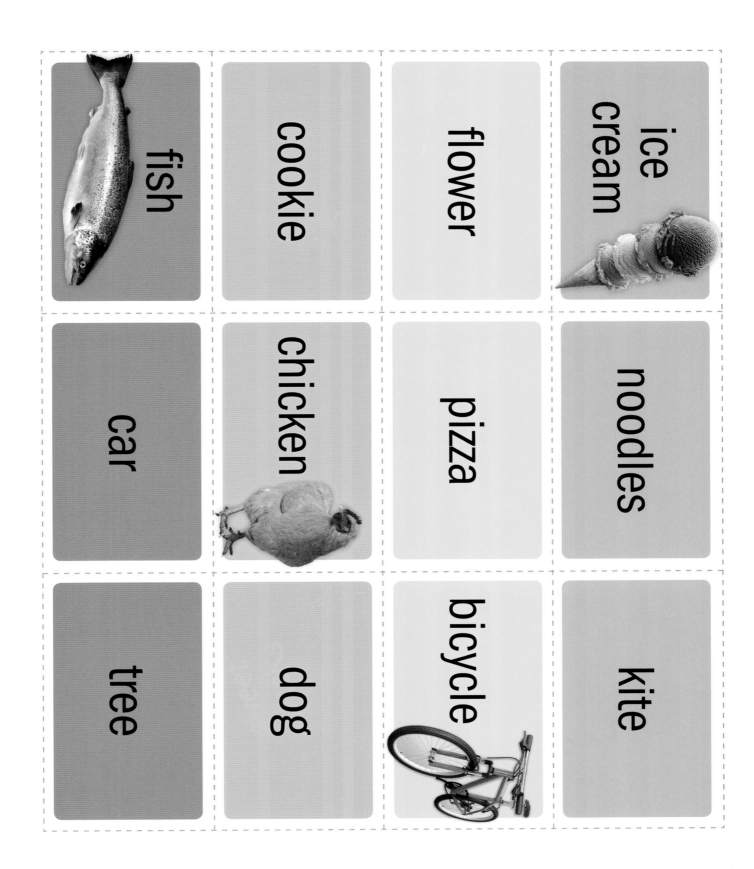

fish

cookie

flower

ice cream

car

chicken

pizza

noodles

tree

dog

bicycle

kite

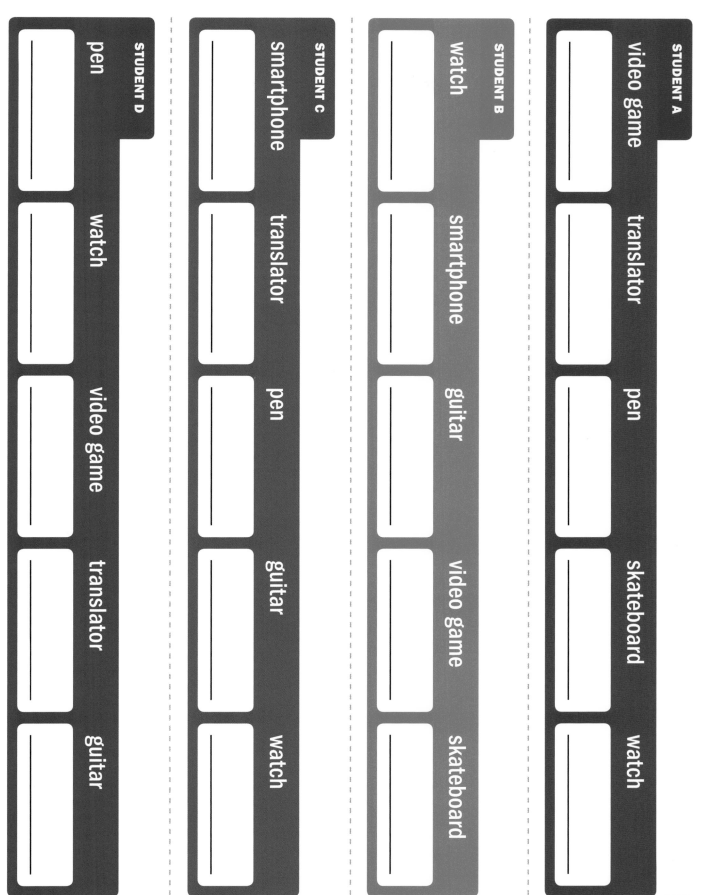

STUDENT A

video game

translator

pen

skateboard

watch

STUDENT B

watch

smartphone

guitar

video game

skateboard

STUDENT C

smartphone

translator

pen

guitar

watch

STUDENT D

pen

watch

video game

translator

guitar

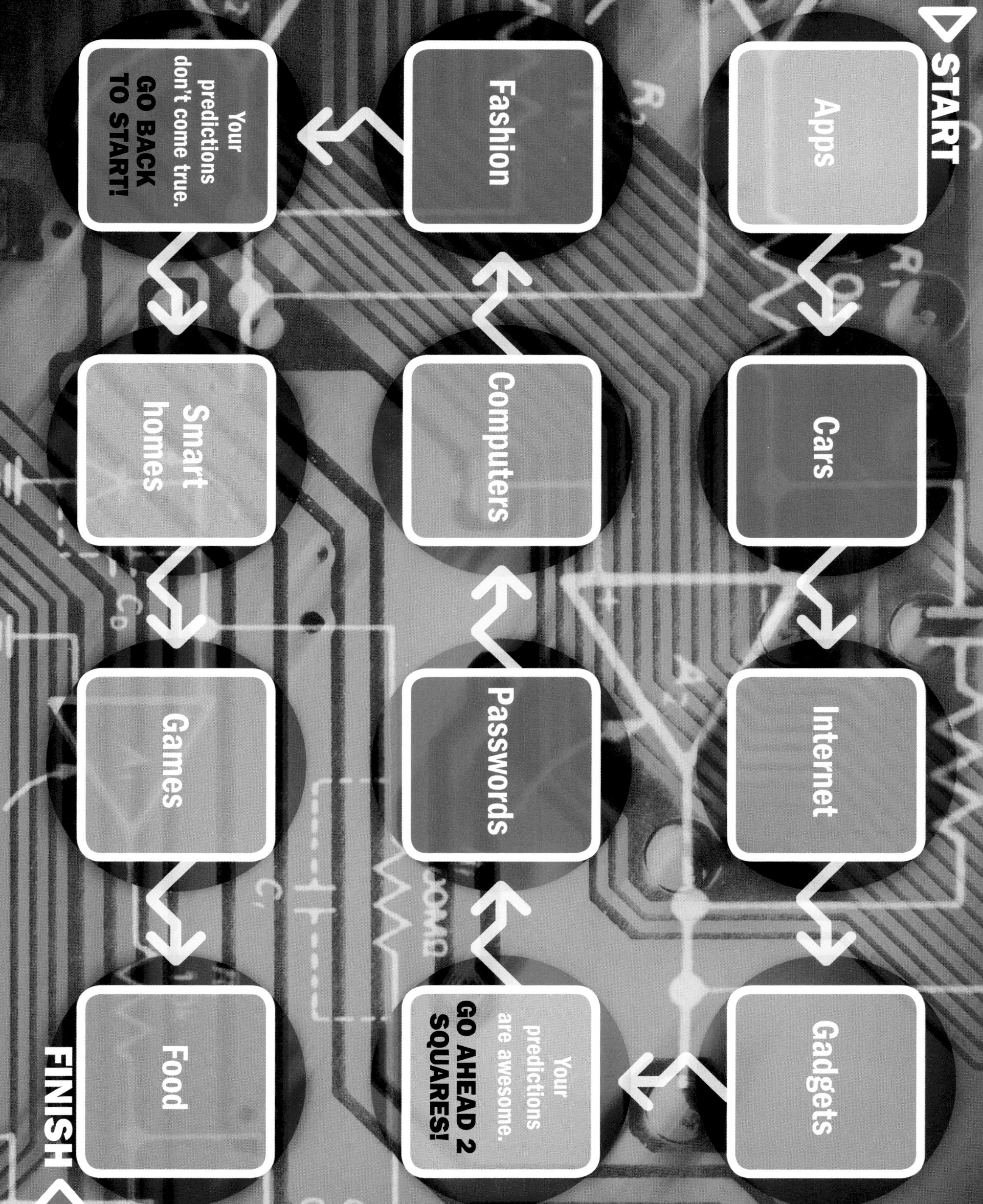

◁ START

Apps

Fashion

Your predictions don't come true. **GO BACK TO START!**

Cars

Computers

Smart homes

Internet

Passwords

Games

Gadgets

Your predictions are awesome. **GO AHEAD 2 SQUARES!**

Food

FINISH ◁

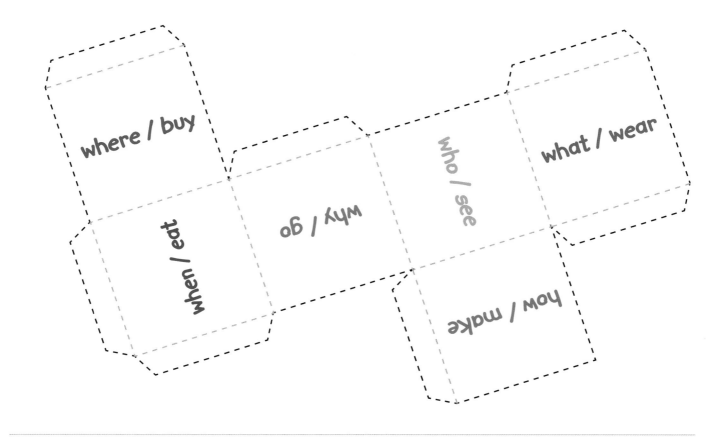

I'm really into . . .	I don't mind . . .	I don't like . . . at all.
. . . is OK, but . . . is awful.	Your Choice	. . . is OK.
. . . is awesome.	. . . is not bad.	. . . is awful.

Will there be . . . ?

There will be . . .

There aren't . . . .

There is . . . .

Was there . . . . ?

There aren't going to be . . . .

There has been . . . .

There are . . . .

Were there . . . . ?

Have there been . . . ?

There haven't been . . . .

There isn't . . . .